Williamsport

"PARTNERS IN PROGRESS" BY
JOSEPH P. LAVER, JR.
PICTURE RESEARCH BY JOHN F. PIPER, JR.,
WITH
THE PHOTOGRAPHIC ASSISTANCE OF
MICHAEL G. ROSKIN

Preferred Marketing
Tarzana, California

Williamsport

FRONTIER VILLAGE TO REGIONAL CENTER

Robert H. Larson • Richard J. Morris •

John F. Piper, Jr.

Overleaf: Downtown Williamsport is captured in this woodcut as it appeared in 1843. Looking east on Third Street, the view features the first Lycoming County Court House on the left, and the Eagle Hotel, the first columned building on the right. Courtesy, James V. Brown Library

Larson, Robert H., 1942-
Williamsport: frontier village to regional center.

Bibliography: p. 172
Includes index.
1. Williamsport, (Pa.) — History. 2. Williamsport (Pa.) — Description. 3. Williamsport (Pa.) — Industries. I. Morris, Richard J. 1947- II. Piper, John F., 1936-. III Title.
The Library of Congress has catalogued the Windsor Publications First Edition as follows:
F159.W7L37 1984 974.8'51 84-21930

ISBN 0-89781-483-5

Preferred Marketing, Publisher

Published 1996
Printed in the United States of America
Second Edition

CONTENTS

Introduction 7

CHAPTER ONE
The Land and the River 9

CHAPTER TWO
Frontier Days 17

CHAPTER THREE
Routes to the World 29

CHAPTER FOUR
Years of Growth: The City 41

CHAPTER FIVE
Progress and Reform 61

CHAPTER SIX
World Wars and Depression 81

CHAPTER SEVEN
Regional Center 105

CHAPTER EIGHT
Epilogue 133

CHAPTER NINE
Partners in Progress 143
by Joseph P. Laver, Jr.

Acknowledgments 171

Bibliography 172

Index 174

"TO OUR STUDENTS"

INTRODUCTION

Left: *Williamsport Recreation Commission developed a number of ice-skating rinks in the city beginning in the mid-1950s, in part because the recently completed flood control system prevented skaters from reaching the frozen river. This view features the rink at the Penn Street Armory in December 1955. Courtesy, Grit Publishing Company*

Williamsport: Frontier Village to Regional Center has been out of print for a number of years. A new publisher is now able to accommodate the continued demand for this publication. They have re-printed this edition leaving the historical section intact with only two caption changes, adding this Introduction, an Epilogue describing important recent events, and making some alterations to the Partners in Progress section.

This page replaces the Acknowledgements page in the original edition which has been retained further back in the book in recognition of the important contributions made by those persons and organizations who originally supplied the data and pictures for the first edition.

The original book was a truly collaborative venture of the three members of the History Department of Lycoming College, who by good fortune continue to teach alongside one another. Although each of us created particular chapters, we reworked them collectively after much discussion. It is difficult even for us to pinpoint credit for a particular theme or interpretation. The Epilogue has not benefitted from such intense discussion. However, it has been shaped in part by the continuous dialogue on local history within the Department, and by the work of Richard J. Morris, Marlin D. Fausey and Michael G. Roskin.

New sources of information about Williamsport and Lycoming County have appeared almost every year of the past decade. Some of them have been very important in helping define particular aspects of local history and deserve recognition but they do not touch directly on topics included in the Epilogue. Among those studies are: Thomas Taber, *Williamsport Lumber Capitol*, Williamsport, Pa.: Paulhlamus Litho, 1995; Samuel J. Dornsife and Eleanor M. Wolfson, *Lost Williamsport*, Williamsport, Pa.: Riverun Productions, 1995; James P. Bressler, *Prehistoric Man on Canfield Island*, Williamsport, Pa.: Presto Print, 1989; and Judith O'Toole, *Severin Roesen*, Lewisburg, Pa.: Bucknell University Press, 1992. Other studies have been important in reviewing the history of the past decade. They include: Charles Haun, Anthony Butto, Michael Gross, and Carl Milofsky, *In Search of the Safety Net: The Migration of Urban Substance Abusers to North Central Pennsylvania*. A Report funded by the Scaife Family Foundation of Pittsburgh, Pa., 1988; and the *1995 Events Calendar* produced by the Lycoming County Bicentennial Committee. In addition, the Lycoming County Bicentennial Committee funded three local projects which gathered data and produced various kinds of permanent exhibits, all now located in the Lycoming County Historical Museum. The projects were: *The People of Lycoming County; The Bicentennial Art Exhibition;* and *Made in Lycoming: The Lycoming County Business and Industrial Heritage Exhibit*.

CHAPTER ONE

The Land and the River

Left: *This view of the West Branch Valley looking west shows two of the major arteries of the Valley, the Susquehanna River and the Beltway. Visible are the three bridges, beginning with the Market Street Bridge, connecting Williamsport on the right with South Williamsport on the left. Courtesy, Marlin D. Fausey and Michael G. Roskin*

The first white settlers struggled up the Susquehanna River in the 18th century in search of new farmland. They saw the West Branch Valley as an area of great promise. Their needs were relatively simple, and their ability to utilize the land was limited to what a few individuals and animals could accomplish. Few, if any, thought about the broader geographic character of the region and how it might affect the future of the communities which they were establishing. As more people came into the valley and the nation began to industrialize, that character became increasingly important. In hindsight, it is clear that geography, specifically the mountains and waterways, played a complex and extremely important role in Williamsport's history. It explains the extent and pattern of the city's development, the reasons for its great period of prosperity during the lumber era of the late 19th century, and many of the problems it has had, and opportunities it has enjoyed since that time.

THE MOUNTAINS

Williamsport is located in the Appalachian Mountains, an old and complex mountain chain that stretches southwestward from the St. Lawrence River in Canada to the Gulf Coastal Plain in central Alabama. Geographers divide the chain into three long bands, each running the entire length of the system. The band nearest the coast, called the Older Appalachians, contains the foothills and piedmont section of the system and lies well outside Williamsport's region. The central and western bands are very important to the story of Williamsport, because the city lies almost exactly on the dividing line between them. The central band, known as the Folded or Newer Appalachians, consists of a series of high-crested ridges and long, narrow valleys which run in the same direction as the chain itself. The ridges range in elevation from 1,600 to 2,100 feet and rise steeply 1,000 or more feet above the valleys which separate them. The most prominent of these ridges in Williamsport's region of Pennsylvania is Bald Eagle Mountain, which, beginning just west of the Susquehanna River opposite Muncy, curves southwest in a great arch for 140 miles. The western band of the chain, called the Appalachian Plateau, is a mass of high ground varying in

elevation from 2,000 to 2,400 feet which extends to cover much of Western and Northwestern Pennsylvania. Its beginning is marked by the Allegheny Front, a sharp rise in the ground which can be seen about six miles north of Williamsport.

Although these mountains have provided Williamsport and the surrounding communities with one of the most picturesque settings in the eastern United States, they have also significantly limited many types of economic activity. Their poor soil, steep slopes, and height make them largely unsuitable for agriculture. Their north-south axis, a barrier against east to west movement of people and goods, caused the entire region to be bypassed during America's great westward migration. Consequently, the region achieved only a limited place in the commercial development that followed. Finally, with the great exception of lumber, the mountains lack sufficient natural resources to attract and support large numbers of people. While the impact of lumber on the economic expansion and development of Williamsport can scarcely be exaggerated, it is no less important to realize the limited duration of that impact.

The continuous effect of the mountains can still be seen on the region's population distribution. Although Pennsylvania has a population of almost 12 million, making it the fourth most populous state in the nation, most of its residents are concentrated in its eastern, southern, and western fringes. The north-central part of the state remains one of the least populated areas in the entire East. As recently as 1970, the Lycoming County Planning Commission reported that 95.4 percent of the county was still undeveloped.

Facing page: *The long ridge of Bald Eagle Mountain reaching off to the southwest is seen from Loyalsock Township. The view shows the dramatic rise of the mountain from the Susquehanna River floodplain. Two of the major local gaps are clearly visible. The first one from the left is at South Williamsport and the one next to it is at DuBoistown.*

THE WATERWAYS

The other geographic feature which has played a dominant role in Williamsport's history is the region's system of waterways. These streams have offered the best and sometimes only routes to and through the area, and their adjacent lands provide most of the fertile soil and flatland that is suitable for agriculture and settlement.

The main components of the water system are the West Branch of the Susquehanna River and its major tributaries: Bald Eagle, Pine, Lycoming, Loyalsock, and Muncy creeks. All but Bald Eagle originate in the Allegheny Plateau region. Together with their subsidiary streams, these creeks drain 5,680 square miles of North-Central Pennsylvania, and except for their headwaters, they drop gently for most of their course. The stretch of the Susquehanna for the 17 miles between Pine and Lycoming creeks is almost level, leading the Indians to give it the name "Long Reach." Many of the subsidiary streams fall very rapidly, some as much as 1,000 feet in a mile, and are thus capable of sending large amounts of water into the system in a short period of time. This has been an important fact of life for the people in the region.

Most geographers treat the West Branch Valley as part of the Ridge and Valley band of the Appalachians, but local archeologist William Turnbaugh, who has carefully studied the area, believes it constitutes a distinct geographic region separate from those to the north and south. Calling it the Susquehanna Section, he defines it as the area from where the river emerges from the Allegheny Plateau to where it curves south around the end of Bald Eagle Mountain, that is from Lock Haven to Muncy, and from Bald Eagle Mountain north to the Allegheny Front. The area is marked by the river, its floodplain, and the terraces and foothills immediately to the north. The valley reaches its maximum width of six miles in the vicinity of Williamsport. This distinction is extremely useful in explaining the attractiveness of the valley for settlers moving into the region in search of farmland. In addition, the mountains provided an inducement to settlement because they act as a shield against cold air moving down from the north. Although most Williamsporters may understandably be forgiven for not appreciating that fact on a blustery January day, the city's winters are significantly milder than towns only a few miles north. It has, for example, an average of 26 fewer days of killing frost annually than Canton, which is only 30 miles to the north.

Thus, if the mountains explain where the people have not

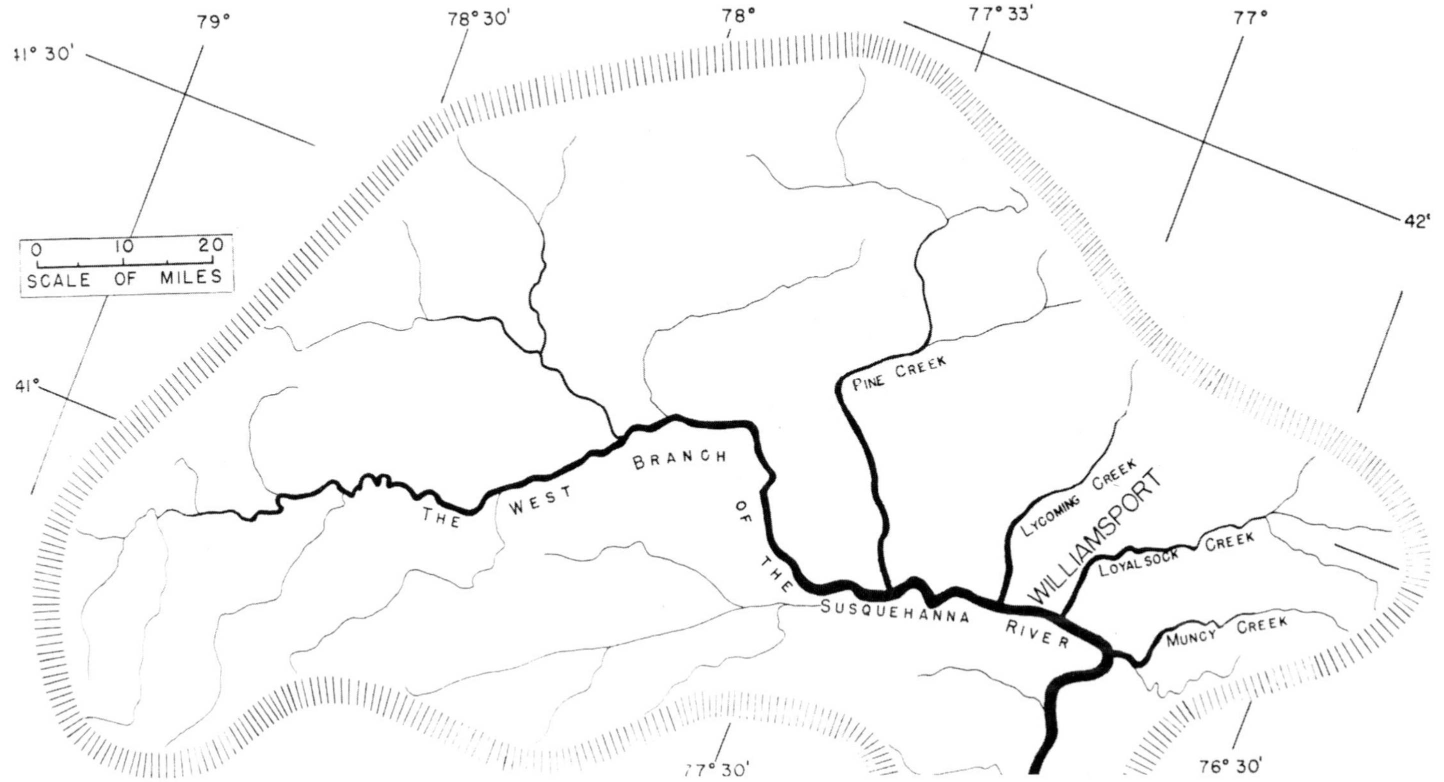

Above: *The drainage basin map of the West Branch of the Susquehanna shows the concentration of tributaries in the vicinity of Williamsport. The size of Lycoming Creek and the extensive drainage of Pine Creek were very favorable to the development and success of the lumber industry. Courtesy, William F. Plankenhorn*

Left: *The Loyalsock Creek Valley is seen here looking north from the mouth of the Creek to the Appalachian Plateau Province. The Valley retains a relatively broad alluvial plain almost until it reaches the Plateau. Montoursville is on the right. Courtesy, Marlin D. Fausey and Michael G. Roskin*

gone, the valleys explain where they have, an observation supported by the fact that 90 percent of Lycoming County's population is concentrated in only 3 percent of its total area along the river.

The waterways and adjacent lowlands present several problems, however. First, they do not penetrate the entire highland region. The West Branch Valley essentially ends at Lock Haven. Lycoming Creek Valley, which reaches north to New York, is a difficult route. Colonel Thomas Hartley, the commander of an expedition up that valley in 1778, likened it to crossing the Alps. Also, however suitable for agriculture the river valley may be, it is simply not large enough to support more than a limited number of people. Finally, as Williamsporters have been regularly reminded throughout their history, there is a flooding problem. Part of this problem is due to geography. The highlands to the north tend to conserve snow longer into the spring when the warm weather causes it to melt quickly. The rapid fall of the small streams of the highlands and the absence of any natural lakes to store the water produce a rapid runoff into the tributaries of the Susquehanna and then in the river itself. When this is combined with heavy spring rains, which are fairly common, the result is flooding of both the Susquehanna and its tributaries.

Floods have regularly disrupted the communications network of the citizens of the Williamsport area. The great flood of 1889 destroyed the Market Street Bridge over the Susquehanna and left its shattered remnants in the river. This scene looks south toward South Williamsport and the Bald Eagle Ridge. Courtesy, James V. Brown Library

Between 1886 and today, the river overflowed its 20-foot-banks 25 times. Fortunately, most of these were not major floods, but in 1889, 1894, 1936, and 1946 the results were disastrous. In 1972 the river reached a record high of 34.75 feet. Although contained by recently completed levees, flooding of the tributaries caused severe problems in many local areas.

In sum, the geographical characteristics of North-Central Pennsylvania indicate that the West Branch Valley was attractive to limited numbers of settlers. Within the valley, settlers were drawn to the area between Lycoming and Loyalsock creeks, because this area possesses the most extensive flatland and the best routes to the outside world.

Williamsport has clearly grown far beyond such a limited scale. A major reason for this was the growth of the lumber industry. Again, this was the result of geography. Many of the same climatic and topographic qualities which made the Allegheny Plateau unsuitable for agriculture made it ideal for the growth of high quality white pine and hemlock which covered the mountains. Moreover, the drainage system of the area was well suited for transporting the logs. The annual spring flooding of the rapidly descending streams was, with the addition of small dams, perfect for carrying the logs down to the creeks and then to the Susquehanna. Once there, it was desirable to turn the raw logs into lumber before shipment to users, or manufacture into wood products. To do this, three things were needed: storage areas for logs waiting to be processed; level land on which to build sawmills and factories; and access to markets outside the immediate region. Williamsport's location, only a short distance downstream from

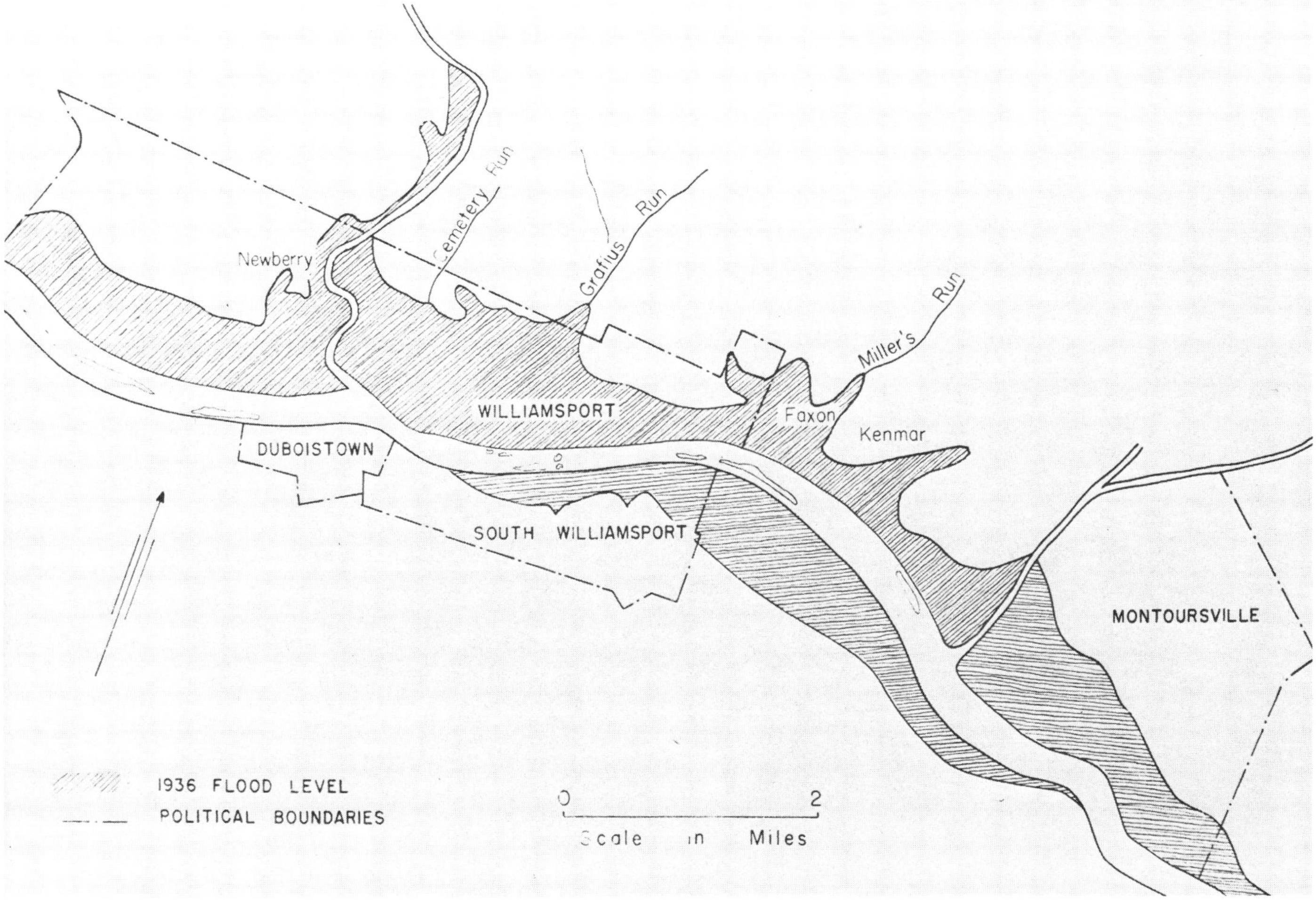

The Susquehanna River crested at 33.9 feet in the Saint Patrick's Day flood of 1936. The map shows how much of the city was inundated. Water rose as high as 10 feet in some industrial and commercial areas of the city. Courtesy, William F. Plankenhorn

Pine Creek at the mouth of Lycoming Creek, provided these three requirements. "Long Reach" provided a stretch of quiet water which could be used for constructing storage facilities. This was enhanced by the construction of a dam to back up the river and by a seven-mile-boom to pen the logs. River islands provided secure anchors for the boom, and a gentle northward curve of the river caused the logs to push against its south bank rather than the boom, so more logs could be stored. Swampy areas adjacent to the river were easily converted into logging ponds to serve as log storage. The widening of the valley plain at this point provided the room for mills, factories, and worker housing. Finally, the canal and railroads provided means of shipping finished products to the major markets of the East.

Thus, the land and the river, which had earlier limited Williamsport's growth, spurred economic activity during the late 19th century. Once the prosperous lumbering years ended, the city's traditional geographic disadvantages reasserted themselves, and go far to explain the problems Williamsport has faced since.

TAILOR
TUESDAY

CHAPTER TWO

Frontier Days

Left: *Russell Inn, built by James Russell in 1796 on the corner of Third and Mulberry streets, served many purposes. It was the first house in Williamsport, the site of early Lycoming County Court sessions, the first inn, and the first tavern. This major city landmark was destroyed in the great fire of 1871. Courtesy, James V. Brown Library*

The earliest settlers in the Susquehanna Valley were the Indians of the Laurentian, Lamoka, Shenks Ferry, Susquehanna, and Iroquois cultural traditions. For the most part, they were hunters and gatherers who flourished in a valley that abounded in oak, hickory, beech, bear, deer, turkey, and fish. The natives originally covered broad expanses of territory in their search for food, but as they became better adapted and developed a primitive agriculture, they reduced the range of their movement to a single large watershed. Generally women and children tended vegetable gardens near the major settlements while the men continued the tradition of obtaining foodstuffs from the forest.

When Charles II of England established the Colony of Pennsylvania and granted proprietary rights to William Penn in 1681, the Iroquois had recently driven out the Susquehanna Indians but had not moved into the area themselves. Instead they had granted settlement rights to various tribes including the Delaware, Shawnee, Chickasaw, and Leni Lenape, who had been displaced from their home areas by whites or other Indian peoples.

Penn required commissioners to extinguish Indian claims before he would provide whites with land titles. The Penn family purchased the West Branch Valley from Governor Thomas Dongan of New York, who had previously been granted it by the Seneca and Susquehanna Indians. The Iroquois protested that the land was theirs by right of conquest, and the Penns, as was their habit, also secured the Iroquois claim in a series of treaties in 1736 and 1768. The area did not attract much white habitation until after the French and Indian War, when a group of officers returning from service asked for land along the West Branch of the Susquehanna. Their request was heeded and soon surveyors were sent to prepare the territory for sale.

By this time the area was the subject of a heated dispute between the colonies of Pennsylvania and Connecticut. Both claimed the land on the basis of vague colonial charters and purchases from the Iroquois. Such conflicting claims among colonies were a common occurrence. Indeed, Pennsylvania had

Members of the North-Central Chapter No. 8 of the Society for Pennsylvania Archeology are shown on a dig on Canfield Island, east of Williamsport on the north side of the Susquehanna River. James P. Bressler, excavation director, records the discovery of a Laurentian burial site, dating approximately 3,000 B.C. Bob Demmien carefully chips away the packed earth in search of artifacts.

similar disputes with New York, Delaware, Virginia, and most notably with Maryland, which was only settled after the surveying of the Mason-Dixon Line. This problem with land claims lay partially with the Indians, who lacked a concept of private property and viewed land as a resource similar to water and air. Thus they believed they were merely granting the right to utilize this resource and saw no reason why various groups could not do so concurrently.

The European concept of private property and the practice of intensive land use made property claims most important to the colonists. The conflicting claims to the area by residents of Pennsylvania and Connecticut led to a series of sporadic raids between the citizens of the two states that marked the first, 1769-1772, second, 1775, and third, 1784, Yankee-Pennamite Wars. The disputed territory encompassed most of northern Pennsylvania including the present site of Williamsport. Battles raged at various times between the Scranton-Wilkes-Barre area and Muncy, about 10 miles east of Williamsport. Conflicts like these in the 1760s and 1770s convinced the British that the colonists could never unite to sustain the strong military effort needed to establish independence. Although the federal government under the Articles of Confederation settled the colonial claim dispute granting the land to Pennsylvania in 1782, it took more than 20 years and a series of complicated

Bull Run Indian Village is shown as it may have looked in about 1400 A.D., when it was inhabited by the Shenks Ferry people. The village, located on Bull Run in Loyalsock Township east of Williamsport, may have been the site of Madame Montour's Village. This diorama in the Lycoming County Historical Museum depicts typical domestic scenes: hunters returning with a deer; women preparing food; a man making projectile points; women hoeing a cornfield; a burial; and children playing. Courtesy, Lycoming County Historical Museum

This model in the Muncy Historical Museum depicts Fort Muncy, which was built in 1778 to protect the Muncy Valley during the American Revolution. The fort was abandoned when the area was invaded by a party of about 100 British and Tories and 200 Indians in the summer of 1779. Although the invaders destroyed the fort, the settlers quickly rebuilt it, but it fell into decay after the Revolution. Courtesy, Muncy Historical Museum

agreements to settle individual titles.

While the claim disputes were raging, the American Revolution erupted. Many settlers moved from New Jersey into the region to avoid the ravages of foraging parties of the American and British armies. This population influx bred conflict between Indians and whites. Throughout American history when the two cultures met, the Native Americans were usually driven west into conflict with other tribes. If they stayed in the east, they were forced into areas far too small to allow them to meet their nutritional requirements. This resulted in malnutrition, disease, and for some cultures, extinction. Many of the Indians in the region, like the Delaware and Leni Lenape, had already been forced west at least once, and so resisted. The British apparently supported this action. They had frozen settlement along the Appalachians in 1763, and were supplying the Indians with arms against the Americans.

This conflict produced two of the most famous events in West Branch Valley history, the Plum Thicket Massacre and the

"Big Runaway," both of which occurred in the summer of 1778. The massacre, one of the first recorded events in what was to become Williamsport, occurred near the present corner of West Fourth and Cemetery streets. It followed a protracted series of raids between the Indians and whites, and resulted in the loss of seven lives, including two men, three women, and two children. During the massacre two other children were taken captive but both were recovered in Canada by their father seven years later. Such attacks spread panic and fear through the West Branch Valley. When a group of British, Tories, and Indians defeated an American force near the Wyoming Valley on the North Branch of the Susquehanna, Colonel Samuel Hunter ordered the settlers out of the West Branch Valley for their own safety. Many settlers who joined the "Big Runaway" were critical of Hunter, arguing the danger did not warrant evacuation. Within a month they began returning to their homes.

At the time of these conflicts in the valley, the site of the original town plat of Williamsport was being surveyed and sold. The first owner was the surveyor, George Gibson, probably the western explorer and Indian fighter from Lancaster County, who acquired title to the land in 1769. Gibson sold it to Matthias Slough, a prominent merchant and land speculator, also of Lancaster, less than two years later. Slough held the land for about 16 years before selling it to William Winter, a tavern keeper whose place of business was located about a mile west of his recent purchase. Shortly before his death, Winter sold the site to Michael Ross, who had been a resident of the area for about 14 years. Ross had served a seven-year indenture with Samuel Wallis, the wealthy surveyor and speculator from Muncy. Apparently Ross learned much from his former master, because almost immediately he sought to exploit the land's location between the two major drainage systems in the inhabited part of the area. He supported the movement to establish a new county in the western section of what was then Northumberland County and requested that 111 acres of his purchase be named the county seat. He was encouraged in this effort by a river survey of 1790 which convinced many that the Susquehanna would become a great inland waterway.

The legislature established Lycoming County in 1795, and the governor appointed five commissioners to select the seat of justice. Four sites vied for the designation, including Dunnstown, Newberry, Jaysburg, and Ross' town. The contest for county seat was quickly reduced to the two locations on the river near the population concentration of the region: Jaysburg, situated south of Newberry at the confluence of Lycoming

Michael Ross, founder of Williamsport, was drawn by an itinerant artist. Born in 1759, he and his mother were living in Philadelphia in 1772 when he agreed to move to Muncy Farms to work for Samuel Wallis. When he completed his indenture in 1779 Wallis gave him 100 acres of land, which likely became the basis of his fortune. He believed in the future of his new town largely because of its river front and he reserved in his deeds all "fisheries and ferries" for himself. Courtesy, Lycoming County Historical Museum

THE COMMONWEALTH OF Pennsylvania

To all to whom these presents shall come, Greeting:

Know ye, That in consideration of the ... money paid by Michael Ross into the Receiver-General's office of this Commonwealth ...

Printed by F. Bailey.

there is granted by the said Commonwealth unto the said Michael Ross a certain tract of land called Virginia situate above Loyalsock Creek on the West branch of Susquehannah River in Loyalsock Township Northumberland County Beginning at an Ash at said River thence by land of Robert Galbreath & Francis Pickley North three hundred and twelve perches and an half to a post thence by said Pickleys land East one hundred seventy six perches to a post thence by land of Paul Weitzell South two hundred & thirty six perches to a post at said River thence up the same by the several courses thereof one hundred ninety two perches to the beginning containing Two hundred Eighty five acres and allowance of six p Cent for Roads &c. Which said Tract was surveyed in pursuance of an Application No 546 entered the third day of April 1769 by George Gibson Who by Deed dated 26 February 1770 conveyed the same to Matthias Hough Who by Deed dated 22 May 1786 conveyed the same to William Winter Who by Deed dated 1 April 1793 conveyed the same to the said Michael Ross to whom a warrant for the acceptance of the said survey issued 1 March instant

with the appurtenances. To have and to hold the said tract or parcel of land with the appurtenances unto the said Michael Ross and his Heirs to the use of him the said Michael Ross his Heirs and Assigns forever, free and clear of all restrictions and reservations as to Mines, Royalties, Quit-rents, or otherwise excepting and reserving only the fifth part of all Gold and Silver Ore for the use of this Commonwealth to be delivered at the pitt's mouth clear of all charges. In Witness whereof Thomas Mifflin Governor of the said Commonwealth hath hereto set his Hand, and caused the State Seal to be hereunto affixed the seventh day of March in the year of our Lord one thousand seven hundred and ninety-four and of the Commonwealth the Eighteenth

Attest. James Trimble Deputy Secy

Thos Mifflin

The deed to "Virginia," the name of the tract of land Michael Ross purchased from William Winter, is dated March 7, 1794. The deed is in the Lycoming County Historical Museum. Courtesy, Lycoming County Historical Museum

Creek and the Susquehanna, and Ross' farm. Ross' town had several advantages, including more high, dry ground nearby for expansion. Ross surveyed the largest townplot and had made the most generous contribution of lots for county buildings. According to tradition, Ross had the support of former Pennsylvania State Senator William Hepburn, who owned land, a grist mill, and a distillery abutting Ross' plot. Hepburn knew that if Williamsport was named county seat the value of his land and the volume of his business would increase. He also had been named president judge of the court as soon as the county was created, but before a seat of justice had been named, and he may have preferred not to cross Lycoming Creek to Jaysburg for court sessions.

Jaysburg long claimed foul play after the commissioners

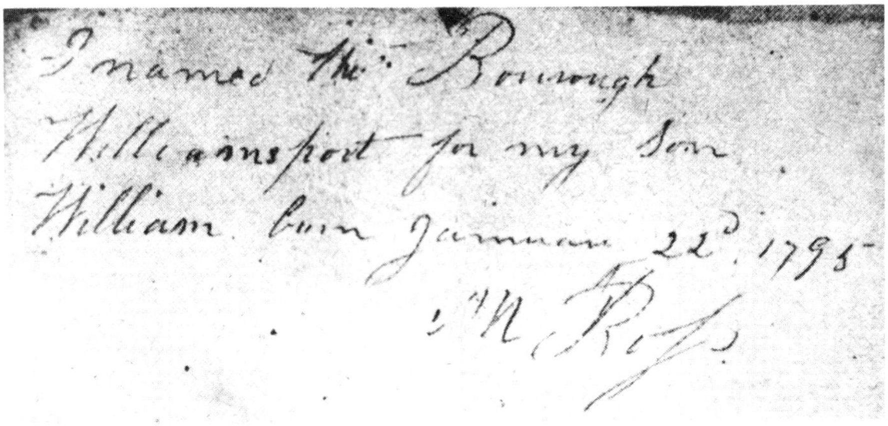
I named the Borough
Williamsport for my Son
William born January 22d, 1795
M. Ross

selected Williamsport as the center of county government. Its residents contended Williamsport was situated on low ground and was susceptible to flooding, and secured an affidavit to this effect. The messenger carrying the affidavit to the commissioners was waylaid by the Williamsport group, provided with ample drink, and awoke to find his saddlebag torn open and the document missing. This is a great tale and it may well be true, but even if the commissioners saw the affidavit they may still have selected Williamsport because the bulk of both town plots were situated 25 feet above normal river level. Williamsport did have a low section that flooded during high water, but this inlet also provided safe harbor for rivercraft, making it an asset as well as a liability. Jaysburg, like many aspiring frontier communities whose future was bound to the acquisition of a county seat, a canal dock, or a railroad terminal, soon passed out of existence. It is now the site of the Williamsport sewage treatment facility.

When Williamsport was designated county seat, it had only one building, the newly-completed Russell Inn. Michael Ross moved immediately to assure his new town's success. On July 4, 1796, he held an ox roast and land auction, selling 16 lots. That same year, he also named the town Williamsport in honor of his young son, William. Still, it took several years to build the courthouse, so in the meantime court sessions were held at Jaysburg, and later a mile west of town at the widow Eleanor Winter's tavern. In 1797 the court finally met in the new county seat for the first time at the Russell Inn. Civil offices and the jail were situated in Jaysburg until 1800. In that year Williamsport became seat of government in locale as well as name.

The 1800 federal and state census data reveal that Williamsport was becoming an economic center. The city contained 131 people, including three or four tavern owners, a

Above: *William Hepburn was born in County Donegal, Ireland, in 1753. He arrived in the West Branch Valley around 1773, achieved a local reputation as a soldier and businessman, and was elected state senator from Northumberland County. It was in this position that he served as the primary force in establishing Lycoming County. Courtesy, Lycoming County Historical Museum*

Above left: *Local historians have long disputed the origin of the name Williamsport. Some believe local citizens named the town for William Hepburn. Others believe Michael Ross named it after his close friends Joseph Williams and William Ellis who surveyed the town. Still others argue it was named for William Russell, a boatman who frequently docked at the lower end of Pine Street. This document appears to settle the issue, for Michael Ross in his own hand says he named the town for his son William. Courtesy, Lycoming County Historical Museum*

The first Lycoming County Court House was built on the plan of the courthouse in Harrisburg. The first court session in the new building appears to have been held in 1804. In 1858 the commissioners, faced with a growing county government, debated whether to expand or replace this building. They had the roof removed so that they could examine the condition of the walls and found them so weakened by age that they had the building torn down. Courtesy, James V. Brown Library

hatter, a tailor, two carpenters, a blacksmith, a tanner, a merchant, a surveyor, a distiller, and two attorneys. As in most nascent frontier communities, specialization was a luxury few could afford. Workers usually produced and sold their own specialty and many practiced several occupations. Robert McElrath, the hatter, for example, served as town jailer and kept an inn for a while. He also cooked the viands for the courthouse raising in October 1802.

One hundred and thirty-one people situated on 111 acres in such an unspecialized economic environment hardly conveys the image of a burgeoning metropolis, but it was 131 more people than had lived in Williamsport when Ross applied to have his tract designated county seat five years earlier. To gain a full appreciation of Williamsport's relative size it is important to realize that Lycoming County had a population density of about one person for every two square miles. The 1800 federal census listed 5,314 people, excluding Indians, in a geographic area roughly twice the size of Connecticut.

As county seat and river way station, Williamsport continued to attract settlers. Its population increased by 86 percent to 244 in 1810, by 156 percent to 624 in 1820, and by 83 percent to 1,140 in 1830. This growth was real but unimpressive when compared to western river cities like Cincinnati, Lexington, Louisville, and Pittsburgh. Indeed, many of the city's early historians lamented Williamsport's slow growth during these years. Michael Ross must have been particularly disappointed in 1810 because he was the largest taxpayer solely because of his assessment for 116 vacant lots. In 1820, two years after his death, his estate was still assessed for 47 empty lots. Surely Williamsport had grown, but it had not achieved the size and significance he had envisioned in surveying the original plot.

Williamsport's mediocre growth resulted from a variety of factors, many arising from its geographic conditions. There were also the rivalries with other river towns like Muncy to the east and Jersey Shore and Newberry to the west, all of which were linked to the north by wagon roads which gave them a trading advantage over Williamsport.

As a result, there simply were not enough people in town to fund projects such as the building of bridges and turnpikes needed to link an Appalachian county seat surrounded by creeks and mountains with a broader economic network. The total tax receipts for the county amounted to $2,393 in 1796 and in 1806, when Williamsport first became a borough, its receipts amounted to a mere $86.70. This was at a time when the county was faced with the immediate expense of building a courthouse, which when completed in 1806, cost $20,417. While the public sector was in tight circumstances, private investors questioned the financial feasibility of establishing toll bridges and roads through the area.

Nevertheless, Williamsporters displayed a burst of civic activity that fostered growth and economic development. They established a newspaper, the Lycoming *Gazette,* in 1801, and secured borough status for the community in 1806 to achieve greater home rule. They ran a stage line east to Northumberland in 1809, a trip which took 14 hours in good weather. They founded Williamsport Academy, the forerunner of Lycoming College, in 1812. They also bridged Loyalsock and Lycoming creeks between 1812 and 1813. Although Williamsporters sought subscriptions to bridge the Susquehanna at various times, a real link to a broader economic world did not occur until the West Branch Canal opened in 1834.

In these decades, Williamsport was in some ways the egalitarian society that historians have often envisioned frontier communities to have been. It was egalitarian in that the leading citizens like Michael Ross, Williamsport's founder, and William Hepburn, the first president judge of the county court, had both risen from obscurity. Hepburn, a Scotch Irish immigrant, first appeared in Williamsport digging a channel for a mill at the mouth of Mosquito Creek before the American Revolution. The background of other affluent citizens is also very obscure, indicating humble beginnings. Indeed, it is impossible to discover background data on William Wilson, the first United States congressman from the city, who served from 1815 to 1819.

Another indication of the egalitarian nature of the society lies in patterns of wealth distribution. The early 19th-century tax books reveal a society where wealth was as equitably distributed as in agrarian areas in Pennsylvania and far more equitable than in more urbanized areas in the state and elsewhere along the eastern seaboard. In 1810 and 1820 the wealthiest 10 percent of the population in Williamsport held between 25 and 30 percent of the taxable wealth, while in Chester County, Pennsylvania, the wealthiest group held as much as 48 percent. In major cities like Boston, New York, and Philadelphia, this group held up to 70 percent of the taxable property.

Williamsport's economic democracy resulted largely from the nature of its migrants and the frontier economy. In Eastern cities shipping merchants amassed huge fortunes and dominated the economic elite in these years, but in 1810 in Williamsport the 10 richest men included two distillers, one of whom also owned a store, three tavern keepers, two store owners, one of whom was the local postmaster, a blacksmith, an attorney, and land speculator and surveyor Michael Ross.

Despite the relative economic equality in the new borough, a social aristocracy seems to have emerged soon after settlement. This is evident from an analysis of marriage patterns among the city's wealthy families. Michael Ross' daughters all married affluent Williamsporters. Elizabeth married Peter Vanderbelt, Jr., son of the sixth wealthiest man in town in 1810, Margaret married James Huling, the richest man in town in 1820, and Anna married Major Charles Low, a fairly successful shoe manufacturer. The second wealthiest man in town, Andrew D. Hepburn, was William Hepburn's nephew. Hepburn married Martha Huston, the daughter of the fourth most affluent Williamsporter, in 1810. The third wealthiest man was William Wilson. After the death of his wife Rebecca, Wilson married Henrietta Van Horne, the widow of Espy Van Horne, a former local congressman. Robert McClure, the fourth in total taxable wealth, wed Mary Hepburn, who was the daughter of Judge William Hepburn. A full analysis of the experience of the ten wealthiest families reveals no instance where a son or daughter of an affluent Williamsporter married poor. Williamsport's society began taking firm shape almost as soon as the town was founded.

Another indication of Williamsport's stability during the frontier era was that a large portion of the town's citizens tended to remain in the county seat. Of the 10 wealthiest men in town in 1810, eight were still present in 1820 and at least one of the other two had died. Persistence rates for others in the town were also quite high during this era. More than half the adult males remained during each of the first three decades of the 19th century, providing a very stable social situation.

The Lycoming County Historical Museum recreated this frontier period blacksmith shop. Peter Vanderbelt was the local blacksmith and may have used some of this equipment since most of it was collected from the local area. Courtesy, Lycoming County Historical Museum

Thus Williamsport's birth and early history were similar to many frontier villages. An entrepreneur hoping to improve his economic situation surveyed his farm into city lots and sought to make it the political and economic center of a region. In 1830 Williamsport resembled an early colonial settlement in many ways. It was geographically isolated, wealth was relatively equally distributed, the population was stable, and the town was rather self-sufficient. However, the city was on the brink of breaking its isolation and of being thrust into a rapidly changing economic and intellectual climate in America during the presidency of Andrew Jackson.

DODSONS DENTAL ROOMS
J.L. MUSSINA.
70 GROCERIES 70
GROCERIES
MERCHANT
20
PER
BOX.

CHAPTER THREE

Routes to the World

Left: *This photograph captures the busy curbstone markets of Market Street north of the Square in the horse and buggy days of the early 1860s. The church spire belongs to the Second Presbyterian Church. The Masonic Temple was built on the site of the Second Presbyterian Church after it was destroyed by fire. Courtesy, Lycoming County Historical Museum*

The Age of Jackson was a time of enormous optimism, when people believed in a benevolent God and a decent, capable humanity. Such an outlook encouraged the democratization of the American political system, producing the growth of popular nominating conventions, popular rather than state legislative selection of the electoral college, and the election of men like Andrew Jackson, who scorned the Eastern aristocracy of wealth and power. The hope of the era also led to the abandonment of established religions in states where such institutions continued, and produced tremendous local church growth throughout the nation. At the same time, church and secular leaders united in their attempts to reform society. Temperance advocates, abolitionists, prison reformers, women's rights advocates, and pacifists all pursued various methods of achieving individual and social perfection.

Economically, this optimism encouraged many to carve existences from the trans-Allegheny West. Others opened factories on a scale American entrepreneurs had hardly contemplated a generation earlier. States and private individuals undertook massive internal improvement projects to bind the nation together and provide the transportation system necessary for the economic growth and development which seemed to be both America's mission and destiny.

In Williamsport the spirit of the age materialized in the work of the abolitionists, the programs of local temperance advocates, the growth of Anti-Masonry, and the birth of new religious congregations. This spirit also produced a pattern of public and private investment that allowed Williamsport to become the commercial center its founders envisioned, and spawned an industrial sector that would nourish economic development in the future.

The most productive abolitionist work in Williamsport was that of the Underground Railroad, a way of helping slaves escape from the bondage of the south to the freedom of Canada. The line was supported by some of the city's most prominent citizens including Tunison Coryell, county prothonotary, and Abraham Updegraff, president of the West Branch Bank, and president of the board of trustees of

Right: *Daniel Hughes was a powerful man, a few inches short of seven feet tall and weighing about 300 pounds. His farmhouse north of Williamsport was the center of "Hughes Territory" on the Underground Railroad. Caves cut into Grampian Hill not far from the farmhouse were used to hide fleeing slaves. The caves have since been sealed. Courtesy, Lycoming County Historical Museum*

Far right: *Abraham Updegraff was one of many successful businessmen who supported public works and contributed to charitable projects. Manager during the early stages of the Williamsport Bridge Company, he was also associated with the Williamsport Water Company. In addition, he worked with the Underground Railroad and Dickinson Seminary. He also found time to be superintendent of the Lycoming County Sunday School Association, and to establish Wildwood Cemetery.*

Dickinson Seminary. Daniel Hughes, an American Indian who was married to former slave Annie Rotch, also did much work for the line. Hughes was a river rafter who picked up slaves on trips to Maryland, transported them to his farm on what is now Freedom Road in Williamsport, and hid them in caves cut into the eastern side of Grampian Hill in preparation for the next leg of their journey, to Elmira, New York. In this effort, the Underground Railroad was aided by Robert Faires, president of the Williamsport and Elmira Railroad.

Closely associated with abolitionism in this period was the temperance movement. Temperance advocates sought to reform society by prohibiting the use of alcoholic beverages, which they believed made people violent and lazy. Perhaps the area's most prominent temperance advocate was John J. Pearce, a Methodist minister from Lock Haven and Jersey Shore who won endorsement of the local Whig and Know-Nothing Parties and was elected to congress in 1855.

One of the major manifestations of political reform was the growing mistrust of the Masons. The Masonic Order was an organized brotherhood which described its mission as "enlightening the understanding, cultivating the mental faculties, and improving the moral virtues of men, and teaching them their duties and relations to each other, in connection with their religious obligations." Suspicion of the Masons was originally based on the members' pledge of secrecy and the belief that they were aristocrats who threatened to control society through a system of mutual rewards.

Anti-Masons, ardent temperance men, were bitter about rumored alcoholic excesses in the Masonic ceremonies. The Anti-Masons were usually abolitionists and egalitarian Democrats who viewed the more affluent and politically conservative Masons with hostility. In Williamsport Anti-Masonry was particularly strong. In 1835 the city supported the successful Anti-Mason gubernatorial candidacy of Joseph Ritner. But the clearest indication of the strength of the movement occurred on June 17, 1829, when a group of Anti-Masons broke into the Williamsport Masonic lodge, which was located on the second floor of the courthouse, and vandalized it, throwing most of the "furniture, papers, records, and working tools" out the windows. So strong was local feeling that the Masons suspended their meetings for 17 years.

Closely associated with the social and political reform of the day was the growth of existing religious congregations and the proliferation of new ones, many of which adhered to liberal views of God and human nature so prevalent in Jacksonian America. The earliest churches in the area were Presbyterian and Methodist Episcopal. The first Presbyterian congregation erected a log building in Newberry in 1792. The Presbyterians established their own congregation in Williamsport on Third

The first Pine Street Methodist Church was erected on the northwest corner of Pine and West Edwin streets in 1826. It was the first brick church in the borough. The pulpit was in the rear of the church and was so high that a child could not see the preacher until he stood to preach. The church was replaced by another brick structure in 1843. Courtesy, Pine Street United Methodist Church

and Mulberry streets in 1833. The Second Presbyterian church was organized in December 1840. The latter body was initially composed of migrants from western New York who belonged to the New School Branch of the church. The Methodist Episcopalians apparently met in the cabin of Amariah Sutton just east of Lycoming Creek around the time of the American Revolution. In 1776 Sutton set aside an acre and a quarter of land for a church, schoolhouse, and cemetery. The congregation was formally established in 1791. The first Methodist Episcopal church in Williamsport proper was built on Pine Street in 1826.

Other churches were formed at about the same time. The Reformed Church was built on West Third Street in 1827 jointly by German Lutherans and Reformed. A Protestant Episcopal church was organized in 1842. The Evangelicals built a church on Market Street near the Railroad in 1845. Saint Boniface Roman Catholic Church was organized in 1853, and Saint Marks Lutheran and the First Baptist churches were built a year later.

The optimism which gave birth to the social and political reforms also encouraged a series of public and private economic endeavors which broke Williamsport's geographic isolation and bound it to a broader economic world. The first and perhaps grandest accomplishment of this nature was the building of the West Branch Canal. The town's first settlers dreamed of a bustling trading center along the West Branch of the Susquehanna. Yet, the river was not easily tamed. It had so many shallows, rapids, bars, and islands that had to be removed or circumvented that it was beyond the means of the settlers in the region to make the waterway navigable for anything but rafts and canoes until the state took an active role in internal improvements.

The state stepped into the transportation business during the 1820s after many false starts and only after the Erie Canal to the north proved an immediate financial success, threatening to draw off much of Pennsylvania's trade. The Erie was paying the interest on its debt even before the entire canal was opened in 1825, and tolls covered the cost of construction within nine years. Equally important, freight rates between Buffalo and New York City declined drastically, leading many farmers in western Pennsylvania to ship their goods north to the lakes and from there to New York City by way of the Erie. Partly as a result, between 1820 and 1830 New York City doubled its population and raced ahead of Philadelphia as the nation's largest port. Hoping to end the loss of its own trade and to emulate the economic development of its neighbor to the north,

Pennsylvania embarked on its own canal system linking Philadelphia and Pittsburgh and sending feeder lines, among other places, along the North and West branches of the Susquehanna River.

The story of the building of the Pennsylvania Canal system is filled with political compromises. Legislators from areas a considerable distance from the main canal voted appropriations only if feeder lines were promised for their districts. The agreement worked well initially, but briefly in 1831 many legislators refused to fund the branch canals. At this point prominent citizens from branch canal towns took action. In Williamsport, William Packer, editor of the Lycoming *Gazette,*

The West Branch Canal in downtown Williamsport is shown in this view looking east from Pine Street toward the famous swinging bridge at Market Street. A packet boat is tied up on the north side of the canal and a wagon can be seen standing on the towpath on the south side. The Exchange Hotel at Market Street was the landing wharf in Williamsport. Courtesy, Lycoming County Historical Museum

and Tunison Coryell, who made 12 trips to Harrisburg at his own expense to lobby for passage of the West Branch appropriation, organized the citizens to place all the pressure at their disposal on the governor and legislature to secure the West Branch funding. They succeeded. Governor George Wolf called a special session of the legislature and an appropriations bill was quickly passed and signed.

William Packer was in charge of construction of the West Branch Canal from Sunbury to Lock Haven. A trench was excavated measuring four feet deep, 28 feet wide at the base and 40 feet at the top. A total of 600 million cubic feet of dirt were moved by hand and wheelbarrow. Locks were built, culverts

William Fisher Packer was one of Williamsport's best known citizens. Newspaperman and civic booster, he was superintendent of the West Branch Canal. He later served Lycoming and nearby counties in the State House of Representatives (1846) and the State Senate (1849), and served all the citizens of Pennsylvania as their governor (1857). He died in Williamsport in 1870. This portrait, an original Currier and Ives, hangs in the Lycoming County Historical Museum. Courtesy, Lycoming County Historical Museum

were established over small streams, and aqueducts over the larger ones. The towpath was graded and finally on October 15, 1834, the canal was filled. Within a few days the first boat passed into Williamsport. The opening of the canal was celebrated by local bands and military groups and large numbers of the citizenry, who turned out for the event.

At the same time Williamsporters actively sought a variety of railroad connections, most importantly a link to a Great Lakes' port to the north. In November 1836 Williamsporters held a railroad convention urging the development of the line from Philadelphia to Sunbury to Williamsport and then to Erie. Governor Joseph Ritner signed a charter for the Sunbury and Erie in April 1837, but construction was delayed by the demise of the Bank of the United States, a main source of the line's funds. The subsequent Panic of 1837 and the lengthy depression that followed kept funds scarce, delaying the commencement of construction until 1852. The line was completed from Sunbury to Williamsport in 1855 and the remainder of the line to Erie was finished in 1864.

During the time the Philadelphia and Erie was being planned, Robert Ralston and some of his friends from Philadelphia developed iron mines and a blast furnace just north of Williamsport and built a railroad line from Ralston to Williamsport to expedite movement of pig iron to the canal at the river city. The line was poorly constructed and mules hauled the freight along the tracks for years because the engine was too heavy for the rails. The line failed financially for a variety of reasons and was sold at auction for $6,000. It was reorganized, renamed the Elmira and Williamsport, and extended to the former city in September 1854. At Elmira, Williamsport traffic was linked to all the important points on Lake Erie and Lake Ontario by way of the New York lines.

While the railroads were being completed, Williamsport's leading citizens were finding other ways to bind the city to the outside world. In 1833 the state legislature appointed Joseph Anthony, James Armstrong, Joseph Wallis, William Wilson, Jeremiah Tallman, William Piatt, Jr., Hugh Donley, Henry Hughes, and William Packer commissioners to sell shares of stock in a private toll bridge across the Susquehanna and to construct a turnpike south to the Union County line. Once the stock was subscribed the legislature passed an act of incorporation and the bridge was completed in July 1849. Two years later, the Susquehanna River, North and West Branch Telegraph Company ran a telegraph line to Jacob Mussina's jewelry shop on Market Square.

NEW ROUTE

FROM

ELMIRA, WILLIAMSPORT, DANVILLE & CATAWISSA:

TO

NEW YORK

AND TO

PHILADELPHIA:

VIA

Williamsport and Elmira, Catawissa, Quakake, Lehigh Valley, and Central Rail Road of New Jersey,

TO

☞NEW YORK,☜

OR VIA

NORTH PENNSYLVANIA RAIL ROAD

TO

PHILADELPHIA.

ON AND AFTER

Wednesday, December 22, 1858,

Passengers for Philadelphia, will take Cars of Catawissa Rail Road at Williamsport, at 10.30 P. M., to Quakake Junction; thence by Quakake Rail Road to Mauch Chunk, arriving at 1.50 A. M.; then take Lehigh Valley Rail Road to Bethlehem, in time for breakfast, and Express Train of North Pennsylva ia Rail Road, and arrive in Philadelphia at 10 A. M.

Passengers for **NEW YORK** continue on the Lehigh Valley Cars to Easton, thence by New Jersey Central, arriving in New York at 11.30 A. M.

RETURNING

Leave Philadelphia from FRONT AND WILLOW STS., at 2.15 P. M., and New York, Pier No. 2 ... RIVER, at 12 Noon.

Arrivi... Willia...

Many new routes to the world opened up for Williamsport in the 1850s. This 1858 advertisement announced a new connection between North-Central Pennsylvania and New York City or Philadelphia. Travelers could reach either of these major port cities in about 12 hours. Courtesy, Lycoming County Historical Museum

With links downriver and beyond the mountains, Williamsporters began to provide urban services for the industries and people they knew would soon arrive. In 1856 two private institutions, the Williamsport Water Company and the Williamsport Gas Company, were incorporated, providing a supply of energy and clean water to the city.

Despite these developments, population growth was slow between 1830 and 1850 when it rose by only 475 to 1,615. But a few years after the canal's completion the city began its transformation to a commercial and manufacturing center. Between 1820 and 1840 the number of people engaged in manufacturing jumped from 83 to 216, an increase of nearly 260 percent, when the population had barely doubled. Between 1830 and 1840 the number of working men aged between 15 and 45 increased 71 percent, while the population increased by only 19

Physician John Crawford came to Williamsport in 1849 after practicing medicine in Cambria, Luzerne County, for 15 years. His home and office are shown in the 1860s (left) and today (right). He organized the Lycoming County Medical Society and served as its president. He also was president of the State Medical Society. He was killed in 1879 while crossing a railroad on the way to visit a very sick boy. The child died shortly after Dr. Crawford. Courtesy, James V. Brown Library

percent. The canal attracted industries which foreshadowed Williamsport's golden age. John B. Hall from Geneva, New York, established a foundry in the city in 1832 which was devoted at first to the production of wood cutting machinery. Similarly, four Philadelphians built the Big Water Mill in 1838, which contained four waterwheels powering four saws to process lumber. Major James Perkins, of South New Market, New Hampshire, who later purchased the mill, built a temporary boom on the Susquehanna River in March 1849 to stop the logs destined for his saws. Following his success a group of businessmen formed the Susquehanna Boom Company and established a boom of their own in December 1849.

Between 1850 and 1860, the coming of the railroads and telegraph, the bridging of the Susquehanna, the development of an array of private utilities, and the establishment of the lumber boom prepared Williamsport for a sustained period of growth. The population more than tripled during the 1850s, rising from 1,615 to 5,664, as many new industries developed. Peter Tinsman opened a steam sawmill in early 1852 and Garret Tinsman and Runyon Woolverton opened another later that year. John and Charles Dodge also established a steam sawmill that year and replaced it with a larger one in 1854. In 1859 Peter Herdic, George W. Lentz, John White, and Henry White formed a partnership and established extensive mills near the river above Center Street. In 1855 George Banger of Philadelphia established the first planing mill and in 1859 John Otto commenced the manufacture of furniture.

While the population grew and industry developed, Williamsport extended its geographic boundaries. The original city was bordered by the river and what are now West Street, Little League Boulevard, and Academy Street. But between 1822 and 1860 the annexation of a series of farms to the north, east, and west more than tripled the size of the community.

This period of growth was fostered by a new generation of Williamsporters led by William Packer, Tunison Coryell, Joseph B. Anthony, James Armstrong, and Robert Faires. Each one of these men was a founder or initiator of two or more of the public works or utilities completed during the 1850s. These men all migrated to Lycoming County and most seem to have risen from relative obscurity but benefited from links to powerful families in the area. Joseph B. Anthony, a graduate of Princeton, studied law with Samuel Hepburn in Milton. After establishing an office in Williamsport, he married into the Grafius family, one of the city's earliest and most prominent. James Armstrong moved to Williamsport from Milton to practice the tanning trade but soon began studying law with Anthony, and later married Sarah Hepburn, daughter of Judge William Hepburn. William Packer, born in Center County, was orphaned at an early age and at 13 was a printer's apprentice at the Sunbury *Public Inquirer.* He served with two other papers before coming to Williamsport at the age of 20 to study law with Joseph B. Anthony. Shortly after his arrival in 1827 Packer secured an interest in the Lycoming *Gazette,* establishing a partnership with Joseph Brandon. Packer married Mary Vanderbelt in 1829, thus associating himself with another of the city's most successful first generation families. Coryell, son of a Revolutionary War veteran, secured a rudimentry education in Buffalo Valley to the south where his parents owned a farm. He then served as a clerk and mail carrier in the area before working for General John Burrows of Montoursville, himself a former Revolutionary War veteran and mail carrier. Coryell seems to have been fairly successful at the time of his marriage. He wed Burrows' daughter Sarah in 1816 and first appears in Williamsport's tax books in 1818 as owner of a substantial house and other land in the city. Robert Faires was born in County Antrim, Northern Ireland, but accompanied his parents to Philadelphia as an infant. His father achieved some political prominence in his new home and became a city commissioner. But while the youth was in his teens his father purchased a farm in Montgomery County where his son worked. When the survey for the canal was being completed, the young man secured a job as an axman but within a few years rose to become chief engineer of the West Branch Extension. Faires married Mary Jane Campbell, who was daughter of the prominent local jurist Francis C. Campbell, and Jane Hepburn Campbell, sister of Andrew D. Hepburn. Judging from the experience of the second generation of Williamsporters, opportunity for improvement was easily obtainable.

Far left: *Major James Perkins came to Williamsport in 1845. Born in New Hampshire in 1803, he learned to be a millwright and a machinist before moving to Philadelphia in 1830 where he employed his trades. In Williamsport he not only bought the Big Water Mill but also built a steam-powered sawmill and the first log boom.*

Left: *Tunison Coryell was involved in many of the efforts to improve Williamsport and develop it as a center of commerce. He lobbied hard for the West Branch Canal, worked to see the Philadelphia and Erie Railroad completed, and urged the government to build a national road through his city. He was cashier of the West Branch Bank and a chief organizer and secretary of the Williamsport Gas Company. In his later years he took an interest in local history and published a book about Williamsport's earliest settlers. He died in 1881.*

These newcomers did not displace the families of the founders. The names Hepburn, Wallis, Piatt, Cummings, Vanderbelt, McLure, and others appear as stockholders on various local utilities and through marriage, continued the lines of the early settlers.

The average workman, however, did not always fare so well during these years because economic ties linking Williamsport to the national economy were not always for the better. The financial Panic of 1837 and the ensuing depression which delayed construction of local railroads seems to have reduced economic opportunity during the 1830s and 1840s. The burden seems to have fallen most heavily on residents who did not own land, because a full two-thirds of the poorer half of the population present in 1830 had disappeared from the tax rolls by 1840. This was natural in an age before unemployment insurance and workfare when the unemployed urban worker had no recourse but to pull up stakes and seek employment elsewhere.

Those who stayed saw Williamsport change substantially during the Age of Jackson. The isolated frontier community had been swept into the mainstream of the changes engulfing America. The abolitionism, temperance reform, political democratization, and religious growth of the age are all reflected in Williamsport's story. The optimism that gave birth to these changes encouraged private and public investment which prepared the city for its golden era. However, the changes of the previous 30 years were nothing compared to what lay ahead.

CHAPTER FOUR

Years of Growth: The City

Left: *Smokestacks and steeples dominated Williamsport in the industrial era. This 1875 view from Vallamont takes in the city from St. Boniface Church in the east to the Herdic House and Philadelphia and Erie Railroad Station in the west. The large building in the left center is Williamsport Dickinson Seminary.*

The bloody turmoil of the Civil War and the Industrial Revolution surrounding it shattered the traditional ways of life throughout America. The war abruptly ended slavery in the South and thrust the federal government into the lives of a people who had rarely felt its reach before. The Industrial Revolution, while increasing national wealth enormously, left a small number of entrepreneurs living in splendor while common laborers toiled long hours over dangerous equipment for minimal rewards. In both of these efforts, the experience of Williamsporters was a microcosm of the American people as a whole.

The firing on Fort Sumter in April 1861 shocked the residents of Williamsport. Although some had expressed sympathy for slaveholders who had found it difficult to secure the return of their fugitive slaves from some Northern states, most now agreed with the Lycoming *Gazette* when it demanded that the rebels "be forced to obey the laws, cost what they may, even to the last man and last cent of the North."

The community responded concretely to the crisis when President Abraham Lincoln issued his call for 75,000 volunteers for three months of service to crush the rebellion. For this call, Lycoming County sent three companies, two from Williamsport and one from Muncy, to join the 11th Regiment of Pennsylvania Volunteers, which was mustered into federal service at Harrisburg on April 24, 1861. The following July this regiment became one of the first to extend its service to three years, and it earned a distinguished reputation for its service with the Army of the Potomic, participating in battles including Antietam, Fredericksburg, Chancellorsville, Gettysburg, and the Virginia campaign of 1864-1865.

Williamsport was also noted for the Repasz Band, a local musical group which had been formed in 1831. It served as the regimental band for the 11th and later the 29th regiments of Pennsylvania Volunteers and played *The Star Spangled Banner* when Robert E. Lee surrendered to Ulysses S. Grant at Appomattox.

These men were joined by other volunteers as new units were formed, and, after March 1863, by men raised through the

Stretching upstream from Williamsport, log cribs looked like strange river forts. When spring's high water brought down the logs, the cribs marked the boundary of a giant storage facility, holding the logs against the south side of the river until they could be sorted and used. Courtesy, Ralph E. Menne

national draft. Williamsporters manned one or more entire companies in eight infantry regiments of Pennsylvania Volunteers, and helped fill the ranks of at least 12 additional infantry and six cavalry regiments. Approximately 9 percent of the county's 1860 population served in one way or another in the Union armies, a proportion comparable to that of the nation as a whole.

The large armies raised by these means naturally required an equal effort on the home front to support them, and in this too, Williamsport and Lycoming County contibuted their share. Troops traveling through Williamsport on the railroad were fed by the women of the town who set up serving tables on Fourth Street between Pine and Mulberry streets. The citizens of the town raised $3,000 for the benefit of local families whose men were with the army, and at least one landlord suspended the rent payments for such families. Ladies aid societies were formed in conjunction with the U.S. Sanitary Commission to provide troops in the field with food and clothing beyond their normal issue. Their efforts throughout the war undoubtedly did much to improve the conditions and raise the morale of the men.

The near unanimity with which the community went to war

MARKING LOGS 2
Logs were marked to identify those of a particular owner.
W&A
308
ME
LHB

Logs were marked before they were floated downstream to prove ownership and ease sorting. This display in the Lycoming County Historical Museum shows some of the marks and the tools used in making them. More than 1,700 log marks were registered by the Susquehanna Boom Company. Log rustlers were common; they simply sawed off the marks and applied their own. Courtesy, Lycoming County Historical Museum

in 1861 could not be expected to last the duration of such a long struggle, and particularly after the last threat of invasion ended in the summer of 1863, partisan politics resumed its course. Despite the efforts of Republicans to brand all Democrats as sympathizers with the South, the latter were able to mount several successful local campaigns and carried the county with a 57 percent majority in the 1864 presidential election. The county even had its own self-styled "peace organ," a local German newspaper called the West Branch *Beobachter* (Observer), but it avoided the bitter internal strife which plagued some Northern communities.

When the guns of the Civil War ceased, Williamsport could

Right: *Peter Herdic (1824-1888), one of the leading figures of Williamsport's industrial era, is shown in this 1860s portrait.*

Far right: *Mahlon Fisher was born and reared in New Jersey. Moving to Williamsport in 1855, he held interests in the lumber firms of Reading, Fisher, and Company and Teneyke, Emery, and Company, as well as the planing mill of Reading, Fisher, and Reading. He was president of the Susquehanna Boom Company.*

justly claim its fair share in the Union victory. To those veterans who had seen extended service, however, the community to which they returned was vastly different than the one they had left.

During the decade following Major James Perkins' construction of the first lumber boom on the Susquehanna, Williamsport's lumber industry grew steadily but slowly. The apparent reason was the limited capacity of the boom. Only certain species of trees could be cut during the summer and very few, if any, logs could be transported down the streams during the fall and winter. Therefore, the lumber industry depended upon the boom's capacity to store a sufficient number of logs to keep the mills working for most of the year. Unfortunately, Perkins' original boom could hold only enough logs to feed a few mills and was not strong enough to withstand a serious flood.

This situation was dramatically transformed shortly after Peter Herdic, Mahlon Fisher, and John G. Reading bought the Susquehanna Boom Company in 1857. The new owners quickly moved to expand their operation. Floods in 1860 and 1861 severely damaged the boom and washed much of the season's harvest downstream, but by 1862 the new owners had devised a strengthened boom employing sunken cribs to which a string of logs was attached by cables. This boom combined the strength and capacity necessary to hold greater numbers of logs and proved itself during the 1865 flood. Eventually the boom was expanded until it ran from the vicinity of the Maynard Street

The Herdic House was part of Peter Herdic's development of the western part of the city. He persuaded the railroad to build its main depot adjoining his hotel and built the horse-drawn streetcar line shown in this picture to provide transportation to Market Street. The streetcar began the same day the hotel opened: September 25, 1865. Courtesy, James V. Brown Library

bridge seven miles to Linden and was anchored to 252 sunken cribs each measuring 20 x 50 feet and 22 feet high. At that point, it could hold 300 million feet of lumber at one time.

The new boom came at just the right time. The Civil War, industrial expansion in the North, and Southern reconstruction created a tremendous demand for lumber, and the invention of new machinery to process the lumber and power the mills greatly increased production capacity. Williamsport and the nation were entering the industrial age.

Much of this change in Williamsport was due to the personal efforts of Peter Herdic. Born in Ft. Plains, New York, in 1824, Herdic was a man of boundless energy and ruthless determination. He came to Lycoming County in 1846 and for several years successfully operated a farm, shingle mill, and sawmill along Lycoming Creek. In 1853 he sold these interests

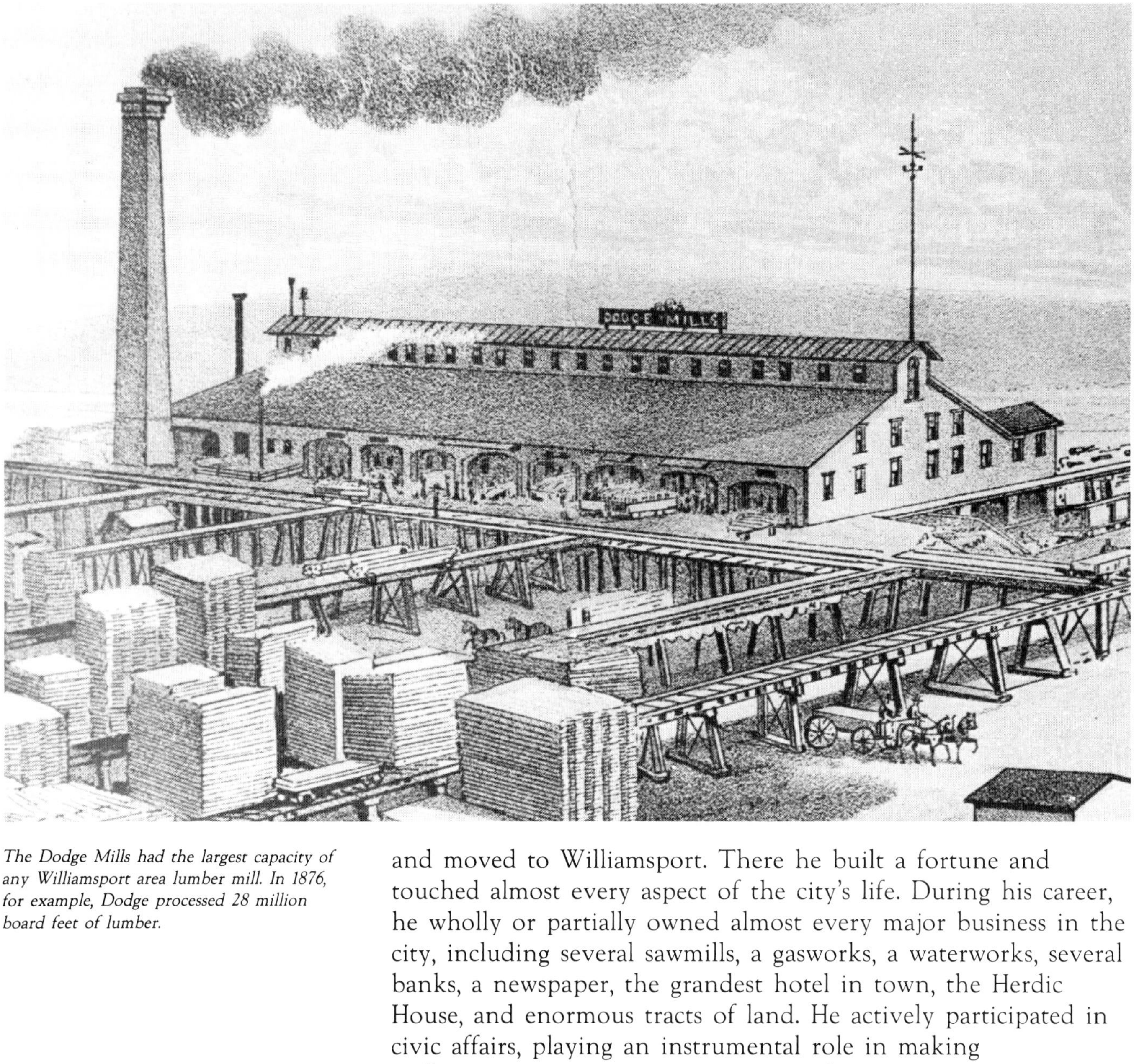

The Dodge Mills had the largest capacity of any Williamsport area lumber mill. In 1876, for example, Dodge processed 28 million board feet of lumber.

and moved to Williamsport. There he built a fortune and touched almost every aspect of the city's life. During his career, he wholly or partially owned almost every major business in the city, including several sawmills, a gasworks, a waterworks, several banks, a newspaper, the grandest hotel in town, the Herdic House, and enormous tracts of land. He actively participated in civic affairs, playing an instrumental role in making Williamsport a city, serving as mayor from 1869 to 1870, and bringing Newberry within its boundaries. He almost single-handedly created South Williamsport by convincing the Pennsylvania Railroad to run a spur along the south bank of the river and then selling lots he owned there to developers.

In all these activities, Herdic was more concerned with the ends he sought than with the means he employed to achieve them. His methods consequently raised more than a few eyebrows among his contemporaries. He was accused of buying his election as mayor. Money was passed freely in the saloons, and when the ballots were counted, his election had cost him

$15 per vote. But he was also a generous supporter of numerous local charities, contributing to the building of churches of all faiths in the city, including its first synagogue. He even sponsored an early form of public works projects to relieve the unemployment problem during the depression of the 1870s by building 800 dwellings in the city. In this effort, he overextended his resources and was forced into bankruptcy in 1878. However one balances his virtues and faults, he was instrumental in the development of Williamsport during the lumber years.

The heart of the lumber industry was of course the sawmills. From their humble beginnings, they grew to number more than 30. Larger mills, such as Guy W. Maynard and Company, B.C. Bowman and Company, and the Dodge Mills, were capable of cutting at least 100,000 feet of lumber in a single day. They were concentrated in five districts along the river, three in Williamsport itself and two on the south bank in South Williamsport and DuBoistown. Their combined record of production is still awesome, In 1862, the first year combined records were kept, 196,953 logs were processed into 37,853,621 board feet. For the next 20 years, production seldom fell below the 1862 figure and was often greater. Altogether, between 1862 and 1891, 31,606,557 logs were processed by the Williamsport mills into 5,545,298,406 board feet of lumber.

Those laboring in the mills found life was often harsh. They worked from 6 a.m. to 6 p.m. six days a week, earning only $1.50 a day and could hope for little improvement in their circumstances. The work was not only difficult, but dangerous and uncertain. Broken saws and flying bits of wood were common hazards. The mill districts were often ravaged by fires which destroyed entire mills and put many men out of work. Since mill hands were not paid for days they did not work, no matter what the reason, the threat of economic destitution was never far from their minds.

In 1872 these conditions pushed the mill workers to strike in what has become famous as the Sawdust War. The mill workers' central demand was a reduction of the workday to 10 hours with no reduction in pay. With the exception of Herdic, the mill owners rejected this demand and eventually had the governor send 400 militiamen to crush the strike. Four strike leaders, including Thomas H. Greevy, a distant relative of a later president judge of Lycoming County, were sentenced to prison. Peter Herdic intervened and persuaded the governor to pardon them. In any event, the strikers were defeated and organized labor in Williamsport suffered such a severe setback that it almost completely disappeared for the rest of the lumber era.

The lumber industry did more than simply provide jobs and wealth. It also served as a magnet to attract many other industries. In fact, of the 6,261 people employed in the city in 1886, only 2,000 worked in the sawmills. Many of these other industries were naturally related to lumber. The most important in terms of employment were: furniture manufacturing, employing 925 workers; metal products with 644 people producing many of the machines and tools used locally; planing mills with 425 workers; the tanning industry with 203 employees. Smaller manufacturers, which also relied on the lumber industry, produced match sticks, toothpicks, wooden toys, and charcoal. In addition, other industries were attracted to the area without regard for lumber. Of these, the most important was rubber manufacturing, which employed 252 people.

Industrial development extended Williamsport's importance as a manufacturing center well beyond the region of central Pennsylvania. Lumber and lumber products were not only sent all over the eastern United States but overseas. The metal industry sent its products equally far afield. The Valley Iron Works sold its products, which included both agricultural and industrial machinery, as far away as Japan and the Ottoman Empire. At the 1873 Vienna International Exhibition, a local firm displayed a steam powered brick-making machine.

This growth in manufacturing was also reflected in the expansion of rail and banking services. By 1886 Williamsport was connected to all major cities in the East by five railroads. Sixteen passenger trains stopped daily at its two stations. The number of banks and savings institutions increased from one before the Civil War to nine by 1890.

Finally, all of these activities led to an enormous expansion of the retail business which made Williamsport the commercial center of all North-Central Pennsylvania. By the mid-1880s the city could boast six hotels capable of housing more than 1,000 guests, 25 dry goods and millinery stores, 95 grocery stores, 13 boot and shoe stores, eight hardware and cutlery stores, 14 drugstores, eight bookstores, seven jewelry stores, and 13 livery stables. The most prominent mercantile establishment was L.L. Stearns, which moved from Jersey Shore in 1865.

The bustling business activity transformed the face of the community. Census figures provide the first indication of change: between 1860 and 1870, the city's population almost tripled from 5,664 to 16,030. The nationwide depression of the 1870s slowed the city's growth so that it only reached 18,934 by

Above: *E.A. Rowley and A.D. Hermance opened their woodworking machinery company in 1875. Growing rapidly, the establishment soon needed these impressive buildings to house it. The company made machinist's tools and all kinds of woodworking machinery for furniture factories and other wood-related businesses.*

Left: *This beautiful solid cherry sideboard was produced by the Mankey Decorative Works in the 1880s. Its Eastlake pattern was ebonized and ribbed with gilt. It represents the high quality of furniture produced in Williamsport. Courtesy, Lycoming County Historical Museum*

1880, but in the following decade it again climbed rapidly, reaching 27,132 in 1890. The national trend toward urbanization was also reflected in the region. In 1860 only 15 percent of the county's population lived in Williamsport, but by 1890 that rate had risen to 38 percent.

The political development of the community naturally reflected this growth. In 1866, largely as a result of the efforts of Peter Herdic, Williamsport was incorporated as a city. Major James M. Wood served as its first mayor. The following year Newberry was annexed to the city through the political slight of hand of Peter Herdic and Thomas Updegraff. A series of petitions regarding the future status of Newberry had been circulated when Herdic and Updegraff secured one or more of them. They clipped off the signatures which they then attached

Above left: *The grocery department of L.L. Stearns is seen as it appeared in the 1870s. Stearns was one of the largest grocery and dry goods stores in the city. It occupied a building at the corner of Market and Third streets and had 16 employees. The store moved to its present location at Third and Pine streets, the former City Hotel, in 1889.*

to their own petition favoring annexation. The new petition was then sent to Harrisburg where it was approved before anyone in Newberry realized what had occurred.

In 1870 Williamsport was one of six cities under consideration as the state capital, and, while it was not chosen, its political influence in Harrisburg was so great that officials there came to refer to the city as "The Everlasting State of Williamsport." The growing political importance of the city was reflected in the construction of a new Lycoming County Court House in 1860 and the completion of a new U.S. Post Office and courthouse in 1891.

The growth of educational, religious, charitable, and cultural

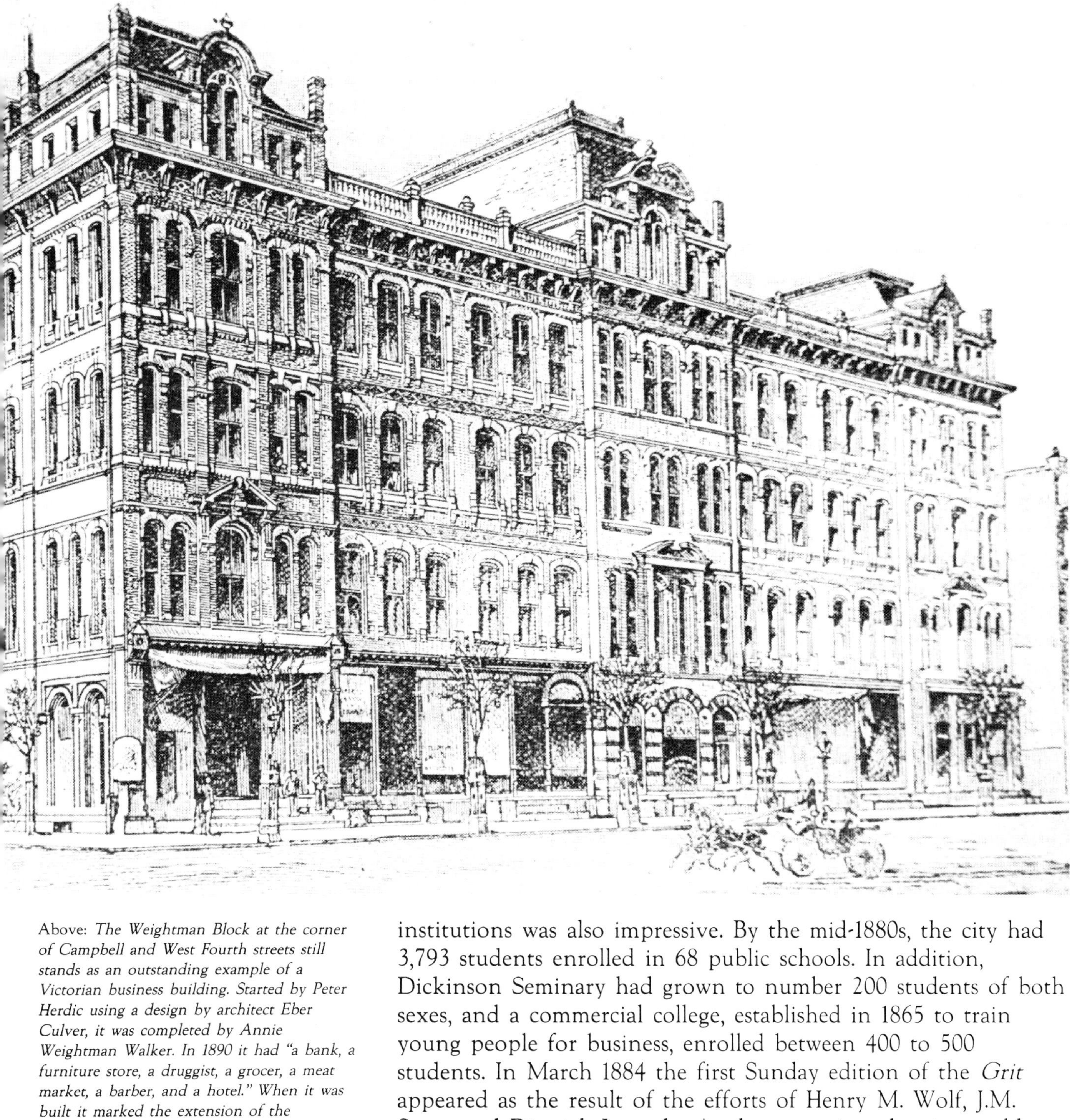

Above: *The Weightman Block at the corner of Campbell and West Fourth streets still stands as an outstanding example of a Victorian business building. Started by Peter Herdic using a design by architect Eber Culver, it was completed by Annie Weightman Walker. In 1890 it had "a bank, a furniture store, a druggist, a grocer, a meat market, a barber, and a hotel." When it was built it marked the extension of the commercial district from the "old town" at Market Square westward.*

institutions was also impressive. By the mid-1880s, the city had 3,793 students enrolled in 68 public schools. In addition, Dickinson Seminary had grown to number 200 students of both sexes, and a commercial college, established in 1865 to train young people for business, enrolled between 400 to 500 students. In March 1884 the first Sunday edition of the *Grit* appeared as the result of the efforts of Henry M. Wolf, J.M. Scott, and Dietrick Lamade. At the same time the city could boast 31 church structures serving every major Protestant denomination as well as citizens of the Roman Catholic and Jewish faiths. Among the more prominent ones built during this period were Beth Hashalom in 1871-1872, Trinity Episcopal in

Left: *Annunciation Roman Catholic Church, dedicated in 1889, still stands at the corner of Walnut and West Fourth streets in the middle of Millionaires Row. A great stone structure, it features a large marble altar and tiffany windows. This drawing, completed around the time of its construction in 1886, shows a high spire similar to the one on Trinity Episcopal Church. During the construction of the spire four workmen fell to their deaths. Father Garvey ordered the tower capped at that height and marked by a cross.*

Facing page, top: *Old Main of Williamsport Dickinson Seminary is seen as it looked in the 1870s industrial era. The west wing (left) was the original building. The east wing (right) was built next, and the two were finally joined by the six-story center unit. It was a private boarding school owned and operated by the Preachers' Aid Society of the Central Pennsylvania Conference of the Methodist Episcopal Church.*

Facing page, bottom right: *The interior of the Academy of Music is pictured as it appeared in an early 1870s advertisement. Prospective patrons were told "the seats are all numbered, and are all raised, so as to afford an entire view of the stage from any part of the house, which is lighted by a handsome chandelier, containing 60 burners." There were a number of dressing rooms for the actors, including a "special room for minstrels."*

Facing page, bottom left: *Dietrick Lamade was a German-born printer journeyman who settled in Williamsport and worked at his trade on an evening newspaper. When he became part owner of the* Grit *in 1884 he published it as an independent Sunday newspaper.* Grit *remained in the Lamade family until the early 1980s.*

Facing page: *The residence of James Gamble (top) is shown as it appeared in the early 1870s when he was serving as presiding judge of Lycoming County. The house, on East Fourth and Mulberry streets, had marble and tile trim in its interior as well as molded plaster decorations. At bottom is the Gamble house as it appeared in 1984. The house has retained much of its original beauty and style, including the window decorations and mansard roof. It has lost its cupola.*

1876, and Annuciation Roman Catholic in 1889.

Medical care expanded at an equally impressive rate. The Lycoming County Medical Society was organized in 1864 with only five members, but 20 years later the city had 40 physicians practicing within its limits. Significant for the times, four of the doctors were women. In 1873 the Williamsport Hospital was established with a nursing school attached, making the city the smallest in the nation to have a hospital. Located in a converted structure on Elmira Street, the hospital quickly outgrew this facility, moving in 1885 to another converted building on Pine Street. Following the 1889 flood, a new structure, complete with all the latest medical facilities, was constructed on Campbell Street north of Louisa Street. In addition, a Home for the Friendless, established in order to care for children and the aged and infirm, was established in 1872.

Finally, the citizens of Williamsport enhanced the city's cultural life with the construction of the Ulman Opera House in 1867 with a seating capacity of 1,000. This was replaced as the center of the city's cultural life only two years later with the construction of the Williamsport Academy of Music. In 1892 the Lycoming Opera House, with a seating capacity of 1,800, became the city's cultural center.

This building explosion naturally caused the plan of the city to be expanded. By the mid-1880s the city's business district (not counting the lumber mills) extended from Mulberry to William streets on Third Street, and from Market to William on Fourth Street. The number of dwellings increased five-fold between 1860 and 1890, from 1,036 to 5,536, and extended northward to the southern edge of what is today Brandon Park. The increased wealth in the city was reflected by the rise of the assessed value of property which climbed from just under two million dollars to more than eight million dollars in the same period.

The most impressive construction occurred on West Fourth Street, which became known as "Millionaires Row." Here the great lumber barons erected mansions derived from the Neo-Classical and Victorian styles, designed to flaunt their wealth and impress their neighbors. They spent as freely on the interiors as they did on the exteriors, filling their homes with grand staircases, polished wood, intricate mantle pieces, lush carpets, velvet curtains, and works of art. Undoubtedly the most impressive of these was the "Million Dollar House" built by Mahlon Fisher in 1867.

This was also the period in which many modern conveniences were established or greatly improved. A gas and water company had been established before the war, but only served the center

ONE WAY

The Youngman estate was built as a summer home in the late 1860s by George Washington Youngman on what is now Round Hill Road. His winter residence was in downtown Williamsport on Pine Street. The estate featured a 24-room Italian Villa brick mansion with cupola, a tenant house, and a large barn.

of the city. When these services were slow to expand, Peter Herdic created new companies to provide gas and water service west of Campbell Street. Eventually the rival gas and water companies merged. Additional improvements followed at regular intervals. A horse-drawn street railroad was established in 1863, the paving of city streets was begun in 1864 although it was limited to the business area, telephone service was established in 1880, and electric lighting brightened the city in 1882. A more unusual service was provided by the Williamsport Steam Company in 1884. By laying five miles of pipe under city streets, it provided heat for businesses and homes up to one mile from its plant. Travel across the Susquehanna River was also improved by the construction of an improved bridge at Market Street. This bridge replaced the earlier one destroyed by the flood of 1865. Access was also aided by the construction of the Maynard Street bridge in 1878. Both bridges continued to charge tolls until 1891, much to the annoyance of South-Side residents.

This surge of growth in Williamsport obviously affected nearby communities although in different ways depending on their location. Montoursville was incorporated as a borough in 1862, South Williamsport in 1866, and DuBoistown in 1878, but the growth of all three was extremely small as Williamsport exerted a far greater draw to people seeking to settle in the immediate area. Lycoming County communities farther away grew at a far greater rate. Jersey Shore, for example, grew from 1,411 to 1,853 between 1880 and 1890, while Hughesville grew

Above: *This mansion was designed by Eber Culver for lumber baron Mahlon Fisher in 1867. It was built on Fourth Street across from the Herdic House and called the Million Dollar House because of what it cost Fisher to construct and furnish it. It was torn down in 1927 to make room for the Young Women's Christian Association. Courtesy, Lycoming County Historical Museum*

Right: *Peter Herdic's mansion in the 400 block of West Fourth Street was designed by Eber Culver in the Italian Villa Style. Built between 1854 and 1855 it was surrounded by lawns which were graced with fountains. Courtesy, James V. Brown Library*

MENS & BOYS CLOTHIER

from 899 to 1,358, and Montgomery from 406 to 770. Although all were dwarfed by Williamsport, the greater growth rate of the latter three indicates that Williamsport acted as a magnet, inhibiting the growth of adjacent communities.

These were glorious years for many Williamsporters, who saw their city's expansion and industrialization as part of a nationwide course to never ending opportunity, progress, and prosperity. Unfortunately, these changes also had their underside. One problem, highlighted by the Sawdust War, was changing employer-employee relationships and patterns of wealth. Early Williamsport society consisted largely of self-employed skilled workers and property was fairly evenly distributed. For example, in 1826 the wealthiest 10 percent of the population owned 30 percent of the property, while the poorest 30 percent owned 10 percent. By 1876 the pattern had changed drastically. In that year, most workers were unskilled laborers working for a relatively few factory owners. The distribution of wealth reflected this change. By 1876 the wealthiest 10 percent owned 61 percent of the wealth, while the poorest 30 percent owned only 3 percent. The Sawdust War reflected the tension this situation produced. While there were no further outbreaks of labor unrest for many years afterward, there was widespread speculation that some of the fires that swept through the mill districts after 1872 were started by workers, indicating at least that tensions were not wholly abated.

A far more serious problem, and the one that eventually doomed the lumber industry, was the lack of conservation. The resources of the vast forests seemed limitless to 19th century Americans who gave no thought to replacing what they had taken. So great was the devastation that one writer described it as "the war on the forests of Lycoming County," a phrase that contains far more truth than exaggeration. The debris from lumbering, limbs, stumps, tree tops, and abandoned logs was allowed to rot and became an ideal source of fuel for forest fires which became an all-too-common occurrence. The destruction of the forests also reduced the ability of the soil to hold water, which in turn increased flooding throughout the area. Land never before affected by high water was now regularly flooded, causing considerable damage to both industry and farming. The most visible result to the people of Williamsport was the great flood of 1889 which inundated much of the city, broke the boom, and carried some 300 million feet of lumber downstream. Although the damage to the West Branch Valley was enormous, much of the destruction was repaired relatively quickly. Unfortunately, the forests could not be replaced so easily.

Facing page, top: *The flood of 1889 crested at 33 feet, one inch, or more than 5 feet higher than the "great" flood of 1865. Every business in Williamsport was flooded, every bridge washed away or severely damaged. The log boom, a major key to the city's prosperity, broke and 200 million feet of lumber swept downstream. On June 1, Market Square was occupied by a single row boat and Market Street with its many food stalls was under water as far as the eye could see. Courtesy, James V. Brown Library*

Facing page, bottom: *When the flood waters receded the city faced a major cleaning task. This view of West Third and Elmira streets shows entire stacks of lumber resting in the middle of the street. Courtesy, Lycoming County Historical Museum, D. Vincent Smith Collection*

CHARLES C. MUSSINA
THE UNION
SODA

CHAPTER FIVE

Progress and Reform

Left: *This bustling circa 1910 street scene was taken on a summer day at Market Square. At right is an open trolley. At right center is the blur of an automobile, too fast for the camera's shutter. Courtesy, Lycoming County Historical Museum*

The late 19th and early 20th century was a time of renewal and modernization in Williamsport. During those years the city enlarged and diversified its industrial base. It modernized most of its urban services like water, sewer, urban transportation, and fire and police protection. The city attracted substantial numbers of immigrants, giving the community a more cosmopolitan and metropolitan flavor. At the same time, many people became increasingly aware of the social and political injustices that accompanied the Industrial Revolution.

Industrialization vastly increased the wealth of post-Civil War America, but much of it fell into the hands of a few. And these men, like Williamsport's Peter Herdic, often translated their riches into power and used that power in ways that seemed to threaten the American tradition of popular government.

Nationally, these concerns over the urban environment and attempts at social and political reform are often referred to as the Progressive Movement. Elements of that movement appeared in Williamsport but not until the city confronted the agonies surrounding the decline of the lumber industry.

In the mid-1880s a few far-sighted individuals realized that the prosperity based on lumber could not continue. The mountains in the region had been cut clean. Soon the resource that had brought Williamsport wealth and national prominence would be in such short supply that the city was in danger of reverting to the small Appalachian county seat and transportation depot that it had been before the Civil War. To encourage industrial diversification, a group of citizens led by Cyrus La Rue Munson, a wealthy lawyer and financier, and John F. Laedlein, a local realtor and insurance agent, organized The Board of Trade in 1885. Within two years the group issued the first pamphlet describing Williamsport's advantages, developed the first city atlas, and enticed several companies, including the Demorest Manufacturing Company, Williamsport Wire Rope Company, H. Diston Manufacturing, and the Royal Braid Company, to locate in Williamsport.

These successes were largely offset by the floods of 1889 and 1894 which broke the lumber boom and inundated old and new businesses alike. The destruction stalled Williamsport's economic

Above: *Williamsport built a new home for its expanding city government in the early 1890s. Designed by architect Eber Culver, built on the former Ross Park, City Hall or the Municipal Building was in use by 1895. The City Hall was expanded with a northeast wing in 1936 and placed on the National Register of Historic Places in 1976. Now the "Old City Hall" is home for various businesses and agencies, including the Williamsport-Lycoming Chamber of Commerce.* Courtesy, James V. Brown Library

life and slowed its population growth. The population which had increased 43.3 percent during the previous decade grew only 5.9 percent during the final 10 years of the century and the assessed property value of the town actually decreased by .4 percent.

This pattern of stagnation in a community for which rapid growth and economic development had become the norm produced another flurry of activity by The Board of Trade designed to revitalize the local economy. In 1900 a committee of 25 members assembled to propose changes in The Board. The Board acquired new offices in City Hall, launched a vigorous membership drive, and worked energetically to attract new industries to the area. All political factions in Williamsport pulled together in this effort. The president of the reorganized Board was J. Henry Cochran, the Democratic leader of the region. The vice president was Samuel N. Williams, the Republican mayor of the city, and the treasurer was James Mansel, the former Prohibitionist mayor.

The reorganized Board of Trade grew rapidly, achieving a total membership of 400 by 1903. This gave it the highest ratio of members to local businesses of any board in the country. The support and enthusiasm paid off quickly. In 1903 alone, seven firms employing 500 men settled in the region. Between 1899 and 1909 the number of manufacturing establishments in the city increased from 142 to 159, while the number of employees in these firms rose from 4,787 to 5,641. During this period the

Above: *Cyrus La Rue Munson was born in New York, and studied law at Yale College, and with the firm of Allen and Gamble in Williamsport. Admitted to the Lycoming County Bar in 1875, he became an outstanding business and civic leader as well as an attorney. He served as president of the Pennsylvania Bar, but was also president of the Savings Institution of Williamsport, of E. Keeler Company, and of the Manson Lumber Company. He was senior warden of Christ Episcopal Church and a chancellor of the Diocese of Harrisburg. Courtesy, Lycoming County Historical Museum*

Left: *The funeral train of President William B. McKinley drew a large crowd to the Pennsylvania Railroad Station when it passed through town September 16, 1901. Courtesy, James V. Brown Library*

average capital value per establishment increased from $60,993 to $88,491 and the value of the products rose from $9,726,000 to $15,348,000. Between 1900 and 1910 the city's population grew from 28,757 to 31,860, a healthy increase of 10.8 percent. The city was again growing and prospering.

In their attempt to attract industry The Board of Trade described Williamsport as a virtual Eden for prospective manufacturers. This placed substantial pressure on city government to provide the services to make this image a reality.

Between 1903 and 1906, the *Grit,* several mayors, and a number of local businessmen urged city government to modernize. The various groups noted that of 83.5 miles of city streets in Williamsport only 6.5 miles were paved. The

Right: *The* Imperial, *built in 1907, was the only automobile ever manufactured in Williamsport. Designed by C.P. VanFerls, a prototype was tested on April 2, 1907, and was said to have reached 60 miles per hour. The Imperial Motor Company built 24 cars, but the "Panic of 1907" tightened credit and the open-body construction hurt winter sales. Consequently, the company went into receivership in 1908. Courtesy, Williamsport* Sun-Gazette

Facing page, top: *The* Grit, *reorganized by Dietrick Lamade in 1884, was a particularly important force for improving community life in the years of progress and reform. The headquarters constructed on West Third Street in 1891 has retained much of its original beauty and grandeur. Courtesy, Grit Publishing Company*

Facing page, bottom: *The First National Bank of Williamsport celebrated its 50th Anniversary in 1913 by building a new home. The opening of the seven-story structure in 1914 was a major public event with thousands of people taking the elevator ride to the roof to see their city from above for the first time. Courtesy, Grit Publishing Company*

community had only 17 policemen. The police had to transport prisoners to city hall in a wheelbarrow because they lacked a police wagon. The city was also without a modern fire alarm or electric system. As a result many called for the establishment of a Board of Public Works run by men of skill and experience to keep streets, sidewalks, and sewers repaired and to establish a garbage collection system.

At the same time, two existing governmental institutions, the Board of Health and the Almshouse, also known as the "poor house," came under close scrutiny. Many citizens attacked the Board of Health because of its handling of a smallpox outbreak. The crisis began when Fred Leederman contracted the disease and was placed in quarantine as the law provided, but the house he was placed in was uninhabitable, the nursing care incompetent, and he escaped twice, dying of exposure on his second attempt. A short time later there were several smallpox deaths in the West End. A city-wide vaccination program prevented an epidemic, but many citizens, including the editors

GRIT
GRIT AMERICA'S GREATEST FAMILY NEWSPAPER
GRIT

FIRST NATIONAL BANK · 1913
MORGANS
AJAX TIRES

Two small children stand in the middle of Park Avenue during its 1919 transition from a sometimes dusty, often muddy, rut-filled road to a paved thoroughfare. The view looks west toward Sawyer Park. The paving stones are stacked, ready for use. Courtesy, Grit Publishing Company

of the *Grit,* blamed the Board of Health's poor quarantine control for the later cases. The Almshouse came under attack when Mayor Seth Foresman called for its repair and expansion "because the crowded conditions ... became such a crying evil that public policy as well as common sentiment of humanity call loudly for improvements."

Of course it would take substantial amounts of money to complete all the projects various groups demanded. Money meant tax increases, which the people were reluctant to pay, and the politicians were reluctant to raise the necessary levies. Many argued that if assessments were made fairly the money would be available. Councilman Michael J. Winters represented these views when he stated, "many small properties are assessed for their full value and some of the valuable properties are not assessed for more than half what they would fetch at public sale." Following a similar call for assessment reform in 1907 by Mayor Foresman, the council established a committee to study the matter and subsequently passed a new assessment ordinance. Almost immediately the assessed value of property shot from

Digging sewers early in the 20th century was not only expensive for taxpayers, but it was also backbreaking work. Courtesy, Grit Publishing Company

nine to 15 million dollars, and tax receipts rose by 25 percent.

The city was now in a position to fulfull many of its institutional goals. During the next few years, 11,000 feet of sewer were laid and 359 sidewalks were repaired. Much of the remainder of the increased revenue was used to retire old debts. Order and organization came in other ways as well. For example, the city adopted a fire code controlling the storage of flammables widely used in industrial establishments.

While the city was working to upgrade its services, the privately-owned street railway was doing the same. The horse-drawn line in Center City was electrified in 1891 and the following year the city chartered six new traction companies including the Vallamont, Citizens, South Side, East End, West End, and Junction. Another line was opened to Montoursville in 1897. In 1905 the small single-truck cars began to be replaced with new double-truck cars. Under the one fare system a passenger could board a car in Newberry transfer at Market Square and travel to Vallamont for a nickle.

Some leaders, like Mayor Charles D. Wolfe, demanded additional improvements. Wolfe called for the appointment of fire and building inspectors, and for the development of regulations controlling the movement of electric current through

Above: *The Vallamont Traction Company stopped at this pavillion in the Vallamont section. Courtesy, Grit Publishing Company*

Left: *This view of Market Street Bridge in about 1910 is looking toward South Williamsport. The South Side Traction Company tracts were adjacent to the bridge. The city boat dock under the bridge was used by small craft as well as the* Hiawatha. *Courtesy, Lycoming County Historical Museum*

Above: *Saint Boniface Church was built in 1875 on Washington Boulevard and served primarily Williamsport's Roman Catholics of German tradition at the turn of the century. This picture was taken circa 1915. The building burned in a tragic fire on December 5, 1972, even as members of the parish were developing plans to celebrate 100 years of worship in it. Courtesy, Lycoming County Historical Museum*

city streets and buildings. He also argued for additional men and equipment for the police department and for the improvement of the city's sewers. Yet, most refused to support these programs.

The state changed Williamsport from the mayor-council form of government to a mayor and non-partisan commission form in 1913, and many local progressives hoped this would facilitate further reform. Instead, Williamsporters used the new mechanism to conduct business as usual. Even though more streets were paved and new storm and sanitary sewers were installed, taxes were cut, delaying many of the innovations demanded by local reform advocates.

By 1914 The Board of Trade added its voice to those of local progressives. It advocated tax reform, a broad range of public improvements, the establishment of a vocational training program in the high school, the establishment of a board of experts within The Board of Trade to give advice to local industries, and the acquisition of factory sites to provide an ideal environment for prospective new industries. Some Williamsporters, including Mayor Jonas Fischer, believed The Board had lost interest in attracting industry, and had become more concerned with improving the industrial environment for those already in the city. The Board disputed this criticism and worked to improve its image and secure its reformist goals. Some of these goals were achieved, but others were cut short as the nation's attention turned to war.

While Williamsport was modernizing, it was also becoming more cosmopolitan as it attracted significant numbers of migrants from central and eastern Europe. Though the largest numbers of immigrants continued to come from traditional areas

Left: *This new high school building was already under construction on the corner of West Third and Susquehanna streets when the Walnut Street high school burned. The Class of 1914 was graduated from the unfinished building. When Williamsport built yet another new high school in the early 1970s this building became the Klump Academic Center of Williamsport Area Community College. Courtesy, Lycoming County Historical Museum*

Facing page: *One of the spectacular fires in city history occurred on April 3, 1914, when the Williamsport High School, located on the corner of West Third and Walnut streets, burned. The fire started in a basement closet and destroyed the building and all student records. Courtesy, Lycoming County Historical Museum*

like Germany, England, and Ireland, more now began arriving from Italy, Russia, and Poland. By 1910 Williamsport contained 2,332 foreign-born people, approximately 7 percent of its total population. Another 18 percent had at least one parent born in Europe.

At this time, certain neighborhoods developed a distinct ethnic flavor. The Germans settled on "Dutch Hill" near Saint Boniface Church, the Gesang Verein Harmonia Society, and Stroehmann's Bakery. Germania Street was one of the lanes which was the home of many recent German immigrants. The Irish lived mainly on the numbered avenues and near Annuciation Church. The fact that Annuciation was founded in 1865 by the Reverend P.F. Sullivan, and that a large statue of Saint Patrick stands to the right of the altar, give testimony to the influence of the Irish in that part of the city.

The Italians settled in the areas circumscribed by Third, William, Canal, and Chatham streets. The Italian neighborhood

Above: *As new immigrants were arriving in Williamsport after 1900, old immigrant families were expanding. The Updegraff family came to the city very early in its history. Abraham Updegraff was a leading citizen in the years before the Civil War. This picture shows some of the family in about 1905. Levi, the black man, was a former slave whose freedom the family purchased. He is buried in the family plot. The woman in the front row directly in front of Levi was Laura Valeria Mahaffey, the grandmother of Mary Winner Stockwell, who is a business and civic leader in modern Williamsport. Courtesy, Mary Winner Stockwell*

Right: *Domenic Troisi is shown at top left shortly after he arrived in Williamsport in 1913. At top right, Domenic examines a coat in his 1935 tailor shop. Hand-tailored quality clothes was his trademark. Domenic and Bernardine Beiter were married at St. Boniface Church in 1920. At bottom they are seen joined by their family on the lawn of their home on their 45th wedding anniversary in 1965. Courtesy, the Troisi Family*

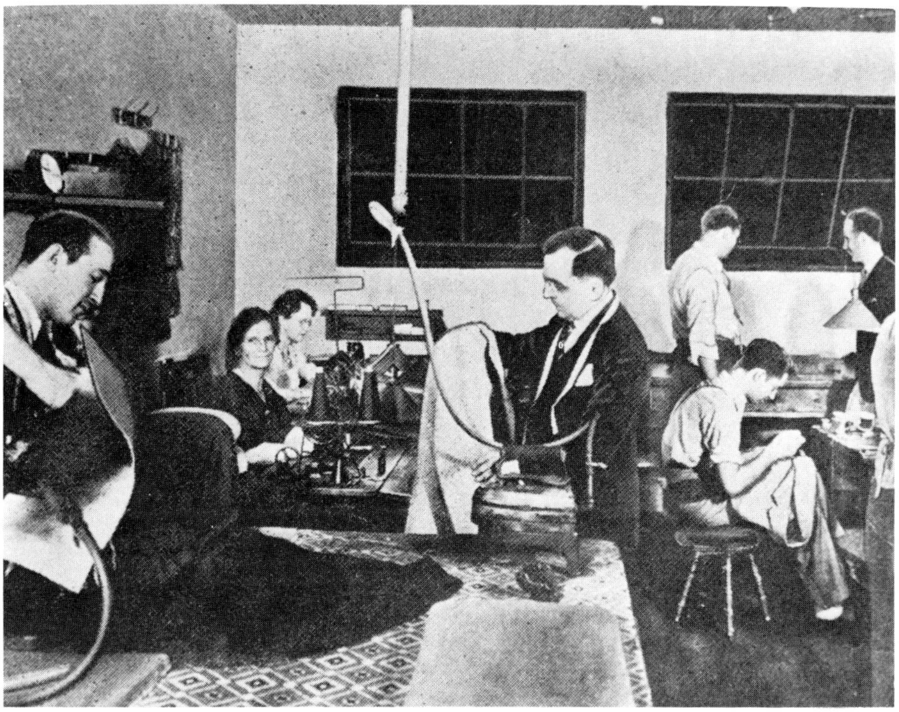

was known as "Little Hollywood." Tradition has it that the name originated because some of the Italian boys were so handsome they reminded people of movie stars. The Italians also founded their own church. Originally they worshipped at Annuciation, but in 1907 Father Domenico Landro, who established seven Italian churches in the Scranton Diocese, came to Williamsport to establish a congregation in Little Hollywood. In 1907 a group led by Father Landro, Americus Vannucci, Michael Chianelle, Peter Cillo, and Peter Nardi launched a fund raising effort to purchase two houses on the 200 block of Market Street which were converted into the First Church and rectory of Mater Dolorosa Parish.

Right: The Knight family has operated a funeral home in Williamsport for four generations. This photograph shows Charles Knight (right) and a brother driving one of their funeral carriages, in about 1915. The view looks west on Memorial Avenue with the Holmes Silk Mill in the background. The funeral home is now operated by John M. Confer. Courtesy, Knight-Confer Funeral Home

The English were scattered around the city, but two other smaller ethnic neighborhoods did develop. Many of the Russian born, most of whom were of Jewish heritage, lived in the East End along Washington Street, Wyoming Avenue, and Elizabeth Street, but several families lived across town along Edwin and Lycoming streets. A Polish neighborhood was located around the intersection of Arch Street and Reach Road.

While ethnic neighborhoods existed, no firm pattern of ethnic segregation emerged. All of these neighborhoods had a mixture of ethnic groups though in certain areas one group predominated. A classic example of this existed on the 700 block of Poplar Street. The majority of people in the neighborhood were Pennsylvania born, but at 704 lived Louis Schneider and his wife Elizabeth who were German born; at 710 lived Italian-born Tony Rizzo and his wife Mary, while across the street at 711 in a boarding house lived Irish-born John Reedy.

Despite the ethnic mix, new immigrants, especially those from central and southern Europe, faced patterns of prejudice and discrimination. One first grade teacher separated the Jews and Italians and labeled them foreigners when class pictures were being taken. The 1928 *Williamsport City Directory* stated "The fact that Williamsport's foreign population is only about 6 percent of the total at once places it in a most unusual class. Since a very great majority of its people are of the real American type, it is easy to understand why Williamsport has achieved a reputation for hospitality and why those whom we have once welcomed are always anxious to return."

Although the new immigrants were facing some hostility, many residents worked to acculturate the immigrant and to improve the living standards of all the working class whose economic conditions were little better than they had been at the time of the Sawdust War.

Much of the economic exploitation of the blue collar worker in America during those years was justified by applying Darwinian evolutionary theory to social progress. The Social Darwinists argued that social progress came as a result of competition among the members of society. Many industrialists used this to justify long hours, dangerous working conditions, and low pay.

Nationally, many groups, including churches, the Socialist Party, and the newspapers, were appalled by the plight of the working class and rejected the Social Darwinian theory that was widely used to justify it. As early as the 1880s, churches began advocating the Social Gospel, which was based on the belief that there was a law higher than that of evolution, the law of love as expressed by God in the Bible. Through private benevolent activity, educational programs, and traditional

Mary Slaughter came to Williamsport after the Civil War. She not only cared for children and the elderly but she was also active in the temperance movement. She is seen here in about 1910.

devotional activity the churches sought to enhance the material as well as the spiritual existence of the workingman.

In Williamsport the local churches worked to secure Social Gospel ends in a variety of ways. An analysis of the benevolent giving by the various Presbyterian churches in town reveals that they allotted from 20 to 35 percent of their donations for such purposes between 1900 and 1915. In addition, the Second Presbyterian Church established a Mission Chapel on Hepburn Street near Front Street, and the Covenant Presbyterian Church established a neighborhood Bible reading class at this time.

The Hiawatha *riverboat is pictured at its landing in Sylvan Dell Park, in about 1910.*

Christ Episcopal Church helped establish an industrial school at Saint John's Chapel in South Williamsport in 1889 and it established a Deaf Mute Class in January 1899. Twenty-five churches joined to form the Williamsport Federation of Churches in 1912. Its committees reveal the type of work it valued. The committees included the home mission, Sunday observance, temperance, social purity, foreign missions, charity, social service, Bible study, community extension, boys work, and finance. The churches also pursued a variety of non-traditional projects to improve the quality of life for Williamsporters. For example, they began a private subscription drive to build the Brandon Park Bandshell in 1912. Although religious services and secular entertainment had long been held at the park, a shell was needed to provide decent acoustics for such occasions.

Residents also established numerous humanitarian enterprises independent of specific churches. Mary Slaughter, born a slave in Martinsburg, West, later moved to Williamsport with her husband where the couple served as caretakers for several local churches. Slaughter was well known for taking children of sick mothers into her home while they recovered. In 1897 she began a home for elderly black women which served the community until 1973. In 1975 the home was leveled and replaced by a low-income housing project for the elderly named in her honor.

While churches and private individuals were working to improve the quality of life for Williamsport's workers, the

D. Vincent Smith is one of the unsung historians of Williamsport and Lycoming County. For more than 50 years, beginning in 1892, he photographed the area, producing an unmatched and not yet compiled picture history. Here he is shown standing on a tractor-pulled wagon train in the Collomsville area. He toured the county on his bicycle, which is visible on top of the wagon. Courtesy, Lycoming County Historical Museum

Socialist Party was working toward similar goals. In the late 19th century, when people were working long hours for a few dollars a day, many began to argue that an undue portion of the wealth produced by industry was accruing to the entrepreneurial class and far too little was finding its way into the hands of the producing class, the machine operators. As a result, many began to argue for government ownership of such enterprises to secure a fair return for the workers. The Socialist movement, strong nationally, had a substantial following in Williamsport. The Socialist Party often had a member on the local city council and in 1917, when Mayor Jonas Fischer retired before the expiration of his term, the council offered the position to Socialist Willard G. Von Neida. Von Neida turned it down. Perhaps the clearest indication of the strength of the Socialist Party in Williamsport can be seen in the Presidential election of 1912. Socialist candidate Eugene V. Debs secured 6 percent of the vote nationally but received 15 percent of the votes cast in Williamsport. Indeed, Debs outpolled the Republican incumbent William Howard Taft by more than 100 votes in the city.

In an attempt to improve life for industrial workers, the press in America castigated all manner of corruption and exploitation, hoping to reestablish morality as the keystone of American life.

In September of 1912 the *Grit* ran stories titled "Little Slaves of the Glass Furnace," "Life Is Cheap in West Virginia Mines," and "Live by the Wages of Sin." These essays criticized child labor in the glass industry, the lack of safety regulations in the mines, and rampant prostitution in various areas of the nation. The paper also ran stories that encouraged humanitarian reform by praising work being done to reduce infant mortality and to educate the deaf and dumb.

Then, as today, working people found relaxation away from their jobs in a variety of ways. They shared in the city's centennial celebration in 1906, joining parades and viewing the displays at the specially-built Exhibition Hall. During the summers they engaged in numerous outdoor activities which culminated rather appropriately on Labor Day. On that holiday in 1912 there were motorcycle races at the County Fair Grounds, canoe races on the river at Sylvan Dell, and a 13-mile bike race from Jersey Shore to Newberry. For those who enjoyed hiking, the *Gazette and Bulletin* described an invigorating 12-hour-hike from Montoursville to Eagles Mere. After a bath and dinner, most of those completing the trek went dancing at the Forrest Inn.

Williamsport celebrated its centennial in 1906 in the midst of a prosperous decade. The Exposition Building, built on the corner of Pine and Fifth streets, was constructed specifically for the occasion. It later housed various businesses and remained in use in 1984. This photograph captures the original building but as the automobiles indicate is from a later date. Courtesy, the Grit Publishing Company

By 1917 public and private groups had done much to improve life in Williamsport. During the next 25 years, wars and depression would test the human and economic resources of the city in many new ways.

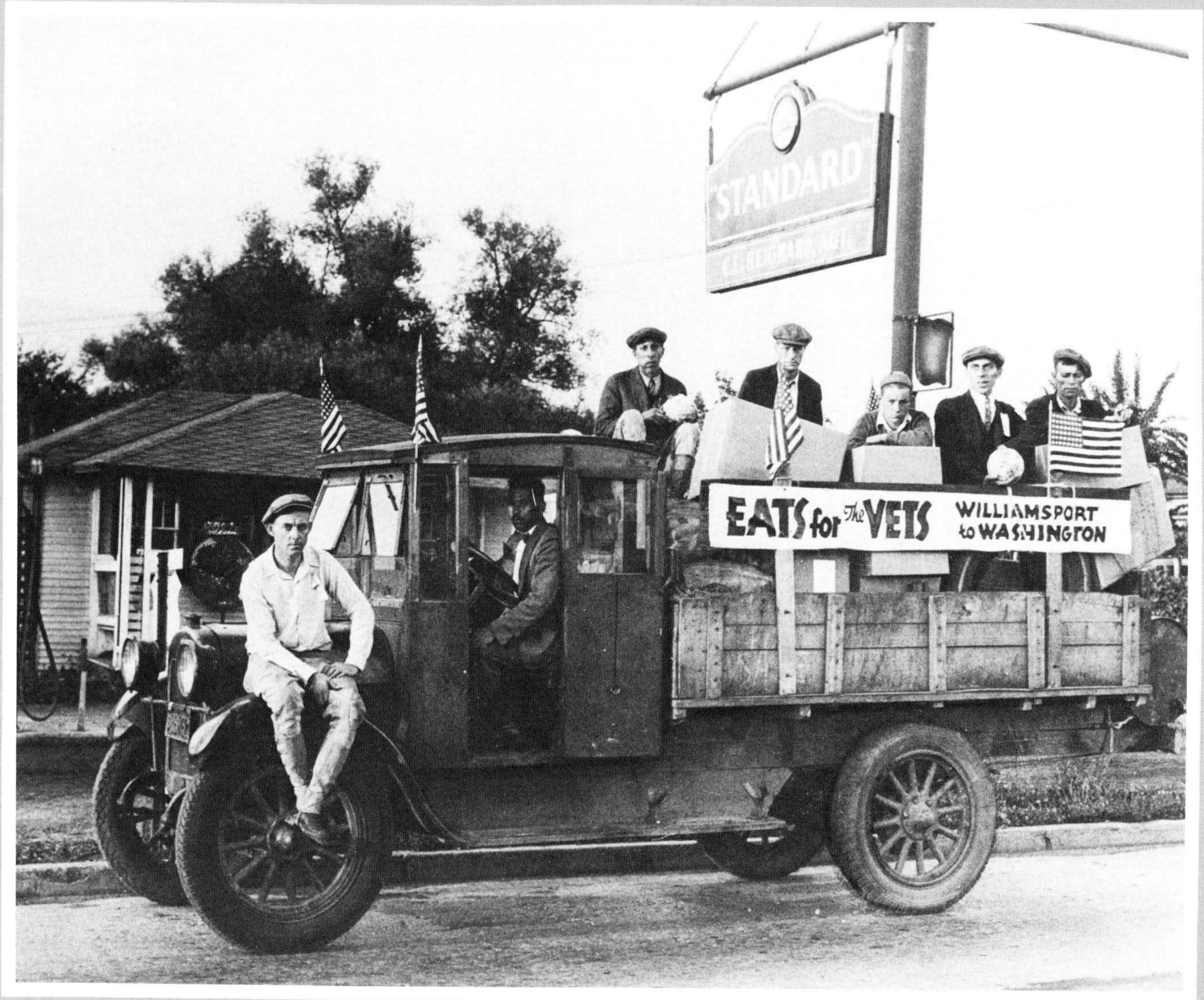
"STANDARD"
EATS for The VETS
WILLIAMSPORT
to WASHINGTON

CHAPTER SIX

World Wars and Depression

Left: *Some Williamsport veterans of World War I were at Camp Marks in Washington, D.C., in the summer of 1932 as part of the Bonus Army, seeking cash payment of their bonus. This truck carried two tons of food donated from the Williamsport area to help feed the vets who joined the protest in Washington. Courtesy, Grit Publishing Company*

The period from America's entry into World War I in April 1917 to the end of World War II in August 1945 was among the most dramatic in American history. Bounded on either side by massive struggles which demanded the fullest utilization of the nation's resources, its middle was marked by the slightly less turbulent, booming 1920s and depression-ridden 1930s. Like the rest of the nation, Williamsporters struggled with these challenges and, in the end, emerged victorious.

The American people who entered World War I did so with the realization that the oncoming struggle would require all their efforts. This was particularly true in the raising of troops. National Guard units would, of course, do their part, but the primary vehicle for recruitment was the national draft law signed on May 18, 1917, which became operational two months later. Williamsport's and Lycoming County's responses were immediate. The local National Guard unit, Battery D, 1st Pennsylvania Field Artillery, was called up on July 15. Redesignated Battery D, 107th Field Artillery, it sailed for France the following year and participated in the final American offensives of the war. Another local organization, the Repasz Band, which had seen service in the Civil War, also was recruited as a unit, redesignated as the Marine Band, and toured the country supporting recruiting and war bond drives.

Most men who served, whether as volunteers or as draftees, did not serve, however, with local units. A total of 3,170 Lycoming County men saw military service. Of these men, 1,296 were volunteers and 1,874 were draftees.

Efforts to mobilize the home front proceeded with equal rapidity. Immediately after war was declared, county officials established a Committee of Public Safety to coordinate all civil and military activity within the county. Eventually, this committee established more than 12 subcommittees to regulate every aspect of community life relating directly or indirectly to the war effort. Among the most important of these were finance, agriculture, plants and materials, fuel, transportation, and civic relief.

Many of the activities of these committees were concerned with conservation, for the United States not only had to supply

NAVY
MEN NEEDED NOW
MEN THE COUNTRY
NEEDS YOU NOW!
STAND BY THE PRESIDENT

Left: *This huge crowd gave a rousing send-off to Battery D as its train moved out from the Market Street Railroad Station in the summer of 1917. Courtesy, Lycoming County Historical Museum*

Facing page, top: *These Navy recruits signed up during the first week after the United States entered World War I. They were sent off as apprentice seamen on April 10, 1917. The Army and Navy both had a record number of recruits from the Williamsport area that week. Courtesy, Grit Publishing Company*

Above: *Soldiers, sailors, marines, and a vast number of other paraders, 10,000 in all, passed under the Victory Arch during the Welcome Home celebration held June 18, 1919. The Arch stood at West Fourth and Hepburn streets. Courtesy, James V. Brown Library*

its own needs, but also quickly became a source of supplies for its allies. Williamsporters had to get used to "meatless" and "wheatless" days, reduction of the temperature in their homes to 65 degrees and, in the last months of the war, strict rationing of goods such as sugar. They also participated in raising money for the war effort through the sale of "Liberty Bonds." Civic organizations such as the Salvation Army, Red Cross, YMCA, and Knights of Columbus helped in the bond drives, as well as many local employers who established programs for their workers to buy bonds in installments.

The purpose of all these efforts was to support the national war production effort, and in this Williamsport also played its part. The most notable local firms involved in this effort were the Lycoming Foundry and Machine Company (today Avco Lycoming) which produced more than 15,000 four-cyclinder engines for army vehicles, and Williamsport Wire Rope Company (today part of Bethlehem Steel) which produced mine nets and cables. In an effort to secure additional contracts, The Board of Trade commissioned its president, Charles C. Krouse, in early 1918 to go to Washington as a representative of local industry. Eventually, the combination of a reduced labor force caused by the draft and increased war orders produced a labor shortage in the city. To help alleviate this, hundreds of women entered the work force, but the labor shortage persisted until the end of the war. By then, Williamsport had added the

Right: *The Curbstone Market was popular in the 1920s, symbolizing the continued strength of agriculture as an area industry. An 1876 ordinance provided for curbstone markets at various city locations, including both sides of Market Street from North Alley to Canal Street. This 1931 photograph shows Market Street north from Market Square. In that year the markets left the streets and moved into the Growers Association Market, a large market house erected at Market and Church streets. Courtesy, Grit Publishing Company*

Left: *A close look at the Curbstone Market in front of the White Kitchen Restaurant, on the west side of Market Street between Third and Fourth streets, was taken about 1920. Courtesy, James V. Brown Library*

FORD
OYSTER BAY
SHOEMAKER

manufacture of shell and shell cases, fragmentation bombs, powder bags, field desks, shoes, and uniforms to their production list.

The summer of 1918 produced another crisis: influenza. This worldwide epidemic, which eventually caused more deaths than the war itself, forced the city to close all schools, clubs, churches, and public places of entertainment, and significantly reduced war production for a brief period. At its height authorities estimated there were 1,000 cases in the city, with another 1,000 in the county. In the end, an estimated one person in every Williamsport home was stricken.

The end of the war brought the inevitable hopes for a better future but also problems of demobilization. The result was a depression lasting from 1919 to 1922, caused by the sudden end of war production and the increase in the labor force due to returning soldiers.

By 1922 the economy was again on the upswing as Williamsport, along with the rest of the nation, entered the "Roaring 20s." This term has special meaning for Williamsport, as the period ranks second in economic growth in the city's entire history, only behind the peak years of the lumber era. Equally significant is the fact that this growth was not dependent upon one industry as in the lumber years, but was now considerably diversified. The metal products industry producing engines and machinery had the largest number of workers, with 3,974 by 1929. Other industries such as leather and rubber, with 1,962 employees, and textiles with 1,335, were also of considerable importance. Surprisingly, the lumber industry continued to be an important source of employment, although its relative position in the local economy had declined considerably. In 1929 there were still six planing mills and seven furniture plants operating in the area with a total payroll of 1,553 people. Overall, the labor force of Williamsport and nearby communties in that year totaled 19,809, 54 percent of which were engaged in manufacturing.

Of the leading firms in the city, several achieved positions of national prominence during this period. The most important of them was the Lycoming Foundry and Machine Company, which changed its name to the Lycoming Mfg. Company in 1920. It produced a total of 57 different types of motors during this period, many of which it designed itself, and became a leading national manufacturer of automobile engines. Indeed, two of the classic automobiles of this period, the Cord and the Duesenberg, were powered by Lycoming engines. In 1928 the company entered the field of aircraft engine manufacture and the first

Right: *Public and private transportation vied for street space on West Third Street in front of the Lycoming County Court House in the pre-Depression summer of 1929. This was a time of transition in public transportation, from the trolleys on the left to the buses on the right. Courtesy, Lycoming County Historical Museum*

Above: *The expansion of the automobile industry created many other businesses, including gas stations. Local artist Larry Seaman created this drawing of the Sinclar Station which was located on the north side of East Third Street as it appeared in 1930. Gas was 16 cents per gallon. The car was a 1928 Studebaker. Courtesy, Larry Seaman*

plane with a Lycoming engine was test-flown on April 5, 1929, laying the basis for the company's later fame. Other firms with national prominence were the J.K. Mosser Company, which had the largest leather sole cutting plant in the world; the Lycoming Rubber Company, which was the nation's leading producer of "Keds," and the C.A. Reed Company, which was one of the largest manufacturers of crepe paper and crepe paper novelties in the country.

One reason for this expansion was the continued easy access of Williamsport to the outside world. The city continued to be served by four railroads, although passenger service was reduced because of a decline in traffic. A major new route was opened in 1921 when the first paved highway, following the north shore of the river, reached the city line. In the 1920s paved roads were extended to the north and west, providing modern connections in all directions. Another modern transportation innovation reached the area in 1929, when the city bought a tract of land in Montoursville and built the Williamsport Airport.

One immediate result of the new roads was an attempt to revive the city's hotel business, which had declined steadily since the turn of the century. In 1920 a group of local leaders formed

Left: *Williamsport dedicated its airport on July 20, 1929. The large plane in the foreground was a Ford tri-motor and was one of the 75 planes at the airport that day. A crowd of 35,000 attended the ceremonies, including Amelia Earhart who flew in for the occasion. Courtesy, Grit Publishing Company*

Left: *The Fire Department's aerial ladder truck is shown here in 1921. The city had some high buildings and new ones were under construction in the early 1920s. The steel structure of one of them, the Lycoming Hotel, is visible in the background. Courtesy, James V. Brown Library*

Right: *Fred Lamade built the Family Theater on Pine Street south of Third Street in 1907. It was renamed the Majestic in 1917 and the Karlton in 1937. The Majestic showed the first silent movies in the area. A number of other entertainments came to this theater, including various vaudeville troupes. The photograph is from 1946. The theater was demolished in 1952. Courtesy, Lycoming County Historical Museum*

the Williamsport Hotels Company and began construction of the Lycoming Hotel, which was opened for business in June 1922. The Board of Trade also sought to take advantage of the new road connections by encouraging tourism through the publication of 50,000 pamphlets titled *The Beautiful Susquehanna Trail.* Although some new business was brought in by these efforts, the results failed to meet the expectations of the sponsors.

The overall expansion of business activity was reflected in the growing wealth and population of the city. The prosperity of the period helped produce better labor relations as local firms established programs such as insurance and pension plans, built plant cafeterias and athletic fields, and organized bands.

Williamsport's population had grown to 44,507 by 1929, an increase of more than 20 percent in only nine years. Real estate values had soared as higher wages enabled many more people to buy their own homes. In one year alone, two million dollars in building permits were issued in the city. Williamsporters were also quick to make the transition to motor vehicles. In 1924, for example, more than 4,000 vehicles were sold locally. By 1927 the city had 22 automobile dealers and repair shops, as well as an annual car show.

In 1929 the Williamsport Chamber of Commerce proudly reported that there were 10,350 dwellings in the city, 70 percent of which were paid for. In addition, public services had reached an all-time high. The public school system consisted of one high

Above: *The Susquehanna Canoe Club on the south side of the river above the Maynard Street Bridge was a popular recreation area. This large crowd was drawn by special late-summer water events in August 1930. Courtesy, Grit Publishing*

Top: *Frank E. Plankenhorn erected this stone entrance at the top of Packer Street in 1926 as one of three gateways to Grampian Hills, a new and elite residential area. The other gateways were to be at the tops of Franklin and Penn streets. The Depression and ill*

health brought Plankenhorn's dreams and his Grampian Hills Development Company to an end, forcing sale of the land. Courtesy, Michael G. Roskin

Above: *Sunset Park was located on Lycoming Creek east of Route 15 between Mill Lane and Roosevelt Avenue. It opened August 8, 1931, and featured many of the amusement rides which had formerly been at Memorial Park. An estimated 12,000 persons attended opening day to see a special balloon ascension. This photograph was taken during opening week from the rocky cliffs overlooking the park and shows Mill Lane and open fields in the background. Courtesy, Lycoming County Historical Museum, D. Vincent Smith Collection*

Facing page: *The Federal Surplus Commodities Corporation provided food for a special Christmas distribution in 1938 to persons on relief rolls in the county. The number of relief cases peaked earlier in 1938 at 4,500, representing approximately 22,000 people. The Pennsylvania Department of Public Assistance distributed the food. Courtesy, Grit Publishing Company*

school, three junior high schools, and 16 grade schools with 268 teachers and 8,664 students, supplemented by two parochial schools with an enrollment of 1,000 students. In 1929 the Williamsport Dickinson Seminary added a two-year college curriculum to its program and changed its name to the Williamsport Dickinson Seminary and Junior College. The Williamsport Hospital had expanded to 275 beds, of which 75 were set aside for those who were unable to pay. Recreational facilities abounded. There were 15 supervised playgrounds, three swimming pools, and numerous athletic fields for baseball, football, and soccer, in addition to facilities for tennis, basketball, and golf. There were seven theaters, eight hotels, and two local daily newspapers with a combined circulation of almost 43,000, plus the nationally-distributed *Grit* with a weekly circulation of more than 375,000.

Williamsport's hopes for continued growth were cruelly dashed by the Great Depression, which struck the nation with the Crash of 1929. Although the stock market crash had little immediate impact on the city, the sharp decline in commodity prices in the early spring of 1930 was quickly followed by the

Right: *The Depression inspired relief gardens. In 1934 this relief garden at the Consistory Plot on Packer Street was one of an estimated 2,500 in the city. A vegetable and canned goods show held in the Armory in August of that year was the first Relief Garden Show ever held in Pennsylvania. The Consistory Plot is now the Lycoming College Athletic Field. Courtesy, Grit Publishing Company*

NOT TO BE SOLD
NOT TO BE SOLD

The Civil Works Administration, which later became the Works Progress Administration, provided the money for many public works projects in Williamsport. This job on East Third Street east of Mulberry Street in the spring of 1934 involved removing the trolley tracks and repaving the street. Courtesy, Grit Publishing Company

curtailment of industrial production and inevitably by rising unemployment. The impact on Williamsport, as on the nation as a whole, was devastating. Between 1928 and 1933, for example, the Lycoming Mfg. Company reduced its payroll from 2,208 to 1,276; C.A. Reed from 771 to 541; and Williamsport Wire Rope Company from 443 to 201. The greatest single blow came in September 1932, when the U.S. Rubber Company, which had employed 1,162 people in 1928, closed its local plant. By 1933 the local unemployment rate soared to 25 percent. The situation was so bad that the Chamber of Commerce noted in its 1933 annual report that some were calling Williamsport "the hardest hit city in the state."

Efforts to relieve suffering caused by the Depression on the local level were not long in coming. In November 1930 a group of businessmen established the Central Emergency Relief Committee to distribute food and clothing to the needy unemployed. It secured funds from the contributions of local companies, organizations, individuals, and workers, many of whom donated 3 percent of their wages. It also held benefit performances and dances. The committee was able to provide $28,000 in goods between November 24, 1930, and April 11, 1931, to about 20 percent of the city's population. The committee attempted to provide temporary work for the unemployed, but, while it met with some success, results were

This swimming and life-saving class met at Mountain Beach in South Williamsport in the summer of 1935 under the sponsorship of the recreation division of the Federal Emergency Relief Administration. Courtesy, Grit Publishing Company

minimal in light of the situation.

While these efforts were a commendable reflection of civic concern, city leaders recognized that the only long-term solution to unemployment lay in attracting new business. Initially, the Williamsport Chamber of Commerce (which had changed its name from The Board of Trade in 1924) led the way in this effort. In May 1931 it hired Charles Krouse to act as its New York City agent to seek out firms that might be willing to move to Williamsport. When such companies were discovered, the Chamber sought to encourage the move by arranging for finanacial incentives such as assistance with moving expenses, local capital investment, a line of credit at a local bank, and rent-free facilities for a limited period. Unfortunately, it met with little initial success, largely because the Chamber's financial resources were in short supply and because many other cities throughout the nation were offering similar incentives. In March 1933 a group of prominent local businessmen, including George L. Stearns, III, and Thomas J. Rider, formed the "Committee of 100" with the expressed purpose of raising capital

Facing page: *Williamsporters gaze at the flood from the First Evangelical Church at the corner of Packer and Market streets in this March 16, 1936, photograph. The Susquehanna River, normally about 1,000 feet wide, expanded to about 7,000 feet. Courtesy, Lycoming County Historical Museum, D. Vincent Smith Collection*

to encourage firms to move to Williamsport. Working together, the Chamber of Commerce and Committee of 100, which merged in April 1937 to form the Community Trade Association, brought 30 new firms with a total of 4,236 employees to the city by June 1941.

Much of this success was undoubtedly aided by a locally initiated and sponsored program of retraining, which eventually achieved national recognition and became known as the Williamsport Plan. Its origins lay in a 1930 survey conducted by the Employment Committee of the Chamber of Commerce, which revealed that while 75 percent of the unemployed in Williamsport were unskilled, 85 percent of those people had adequate educational background to become skilled or semi-skilled workers with the proper training. Moreover, the survey revealed that despite the high unemployment rate, there were shortages of skilled workers in many shops. The Williamsport Plan was designed to take the maximum advantage of the potential which this situation offered. Local firms were surveyed to determine exactly what type of skilled workers they required. Unemployed workers were then screened to determine their suitability for training in these skills, provided with the necessary training, and then placed with these firms. Much of the success of this plan was due to George H. Parkes, director of the vocational department at Williamsport High School, who actually designed the training program and put it into practice. Starting with virtually nothing, he salvaged equipment from local junkyards and obtained donations of unused equipment from local plants. By 1933 the school, known as the Williamsport Retraining School, had grown, and needed larger facilities, so a new building was constructed mostly by students, on West Third Street at Park Street. By 1940 it had trained and placed some 4,000 people, more than half of whom had been on relief rolls.

These efforts to restore prosperity were necessary for the long-term recovery of Williamsport, but they were of little help for many of its citizens who measured their survival in the short term. For these people, relief only came with the arrival of the presidency of Franklin D. Roosevelt and the New Deal. In particular, the Works Progress Administration, known as the WPA, not only provided necessary jobs for the unemployed, but also established many public works projects which benefited the entire community. Between July 1, 1935, and June 30, 1938, the WPA provided $5,343,170 in work relief for Lycoming County, of which more than 90 percent went for wages. At its peak, it provided employment for 3,637 persons in a wide range of activities. New schools were built while others were rehabilitated or received additions, roads were paved and otherwise improved, and a runway and hanger were constructed at the airport in Montoursville.

Just as the first signs of recovery appeared, however, disaster struck again, this time in the form of a flood. The winter of 1935-1936 had been particularly severe, with temperatures close to zero for many weeks and heavy snowfalls in the mountains. Then in March the temperature suddenly turned warm and it began to rain heavily. During the night of March 18, the Susquehanna River crested at 33.9 feet. The results were devastating. Two thirds of the city, including most of the business and industrial districts, were inundated. At its height, the water swept through the city with such force that telephone

KELLY
TRUCK TIRES

J. C. PENNEY COMPANY
Drugs

Left: *The flood waters were nearly 10 feet deep on William Street south of Third Street when fire erupted at the Wakenhut Building on March 18. The fire burned the entire block down to water level. Eighteen people were rescued from the buildings without loss of life. Fire equipment had been moved to Brandon Park to save it from the flood. Courtesy, Grit Publishing Company*

Left: *West Fourth Street is pictured looking east toward Pine Street during the flood of 1936. Almost every business in the city suffered damage. Courtesy, James V. Brown Library*

and telegraph lines were cut, railroad tracks were wiped out, and cars were overturned. Miraculously, only three people in the county lost their lives, undoubtedly a tribute to the early warnings and guidance of the community's civic leaders. As the waters receded, residents immediately began repairing the damage aided by local and federal relief agencies and began to study the possibility of constructing levees for protection against future floods.

By 1940 Williamsporters could thus feel that they had weathered the worst that nature and the economy could deal them. Yet, the cost was high. In fact, for the first time in its history, the population of Williamsport actually declined during this decade, from 45,729 in 1930 to 44,355 in 1940, a loss of almost 1,400 people, while during the same period the population of Lycoming County rose by only 200.

The Japanese attack on Pearl Harbor, which brought the United States into World War II, shocked the American people, uniting them in their resolve for total victory. Williamsport was involved in the struggle from the very beginning. One local serviceman stationed at Pearl Harbor, Joseph L. Lockard, observed the approaching Japanese planes on a primitive radar set, but his warnings were ignored by his superiors.

Williamsporters entered the war with the same determination and willingness to sacrifice that had marked their participation in the nation's earlier wars. Many young men served in the 109th Infantry Regiment of the 28th Infantry Division of the Pennsylvania National Guard. Following two years of training in the United States and Great Britian, the division landed in France shortly after D-Day and were among the first American troops to enter Paris in August 1944. In November they participated in the battle for Huertgen Forest where they suffered severe casualties in what many consider to be the most savage fighting the United States Army ever experienced in Europe. Afterwards they were transferred to a "quiet" sector of the front, the Ardennes. When the Germans attacked in what became known as the Battle of the Bulge, the division was shattered by an overwhelming superiority of numbers, but nonetheless helped slow the German tide until reinforcements arrived.

Meanwhile, Williamsporters at home were experiencing a degree of government control that greatly surpassed their earlier experiences. Rationing began within weeks of the start of the war. Automobile tires topped the list. In order to obtain new tires, it was necessary to receive approval from a county rationing board composed of four local citizens and, except for

The Lycoming engine, the R-680, 295 h.p., powered the twin engine Beech Trainer. These were being readied for delivery to army air force schools in August 1943. Courtesy, Grit Publishing Company

individuals who were in specified fields, such as physicians, this was extremely difficult. Moreover, the board decided early to publish the names of all individuals who received tires in the local newspapers to allay charges of favoritism. In May 1942 sugar rationing went into effect. In a three-day period, almost 45,000 families registered at city schools for their cards. The same month, gas rationing was announced, and non-essential vehicles were allotted two gallons per week. The following January pleasure driving was banned and local officials were given the unpopular task of checking the presence of cars at local amusement spots.

Williamsporters also contributed their share to war production and, because of the growing diversification of industry, did so in more ways than ever before. The largest private employer in the area remained the Lycoming Mfg. Company, which concentrated on building parts and engines for aircraft and tanks. At its peak, it turned out 600 engines a month, plus parts for planes such as the B-29 and P-51 Mustang.

Local industries employed many women during World War II. There were six times as many women at the Lycoming Division of the Aviation Corporation as there had been in World War I. Those pictured here in July 1943, include, from left, June Schauer, Florence Haines, Lois Livermore, Marie Allison, Shirley Miller, and Lois Messick. Courtesy, Grit Publishing Company

Other firms contributed in an enormous variety of ways, each designed to take advantage of their particular skills in civilian production. The Bethlehem Steel plant (formerly the Williamsport Wire Rope Company) made wire rope for submarine nets; Darling Valve and Manufacturing Company made 75mm and 105mm artillery shells, five-inch rockets, and steel valves for ships and landing craft; Sylvania Electric Products Company, Inc., produced radio tubes and radar equipment, and Holmes Silk Mill made parachutes. Williamsport Furniture Company made cots, lifeboats, bunk beds, and boxes for shipping artillery shells, while C.A. Reed made, among other things, small parachutes for fragmentation bombs. Even the lumber industry revived somewhat as 310 million board feet of finished goods were produced during the war years.

In short, Williamsport's contributions to the final victory were the result of a major community effort which left virtually no one untouched. It was a solid foundation on which to build what most were certain would be a better postwar world.

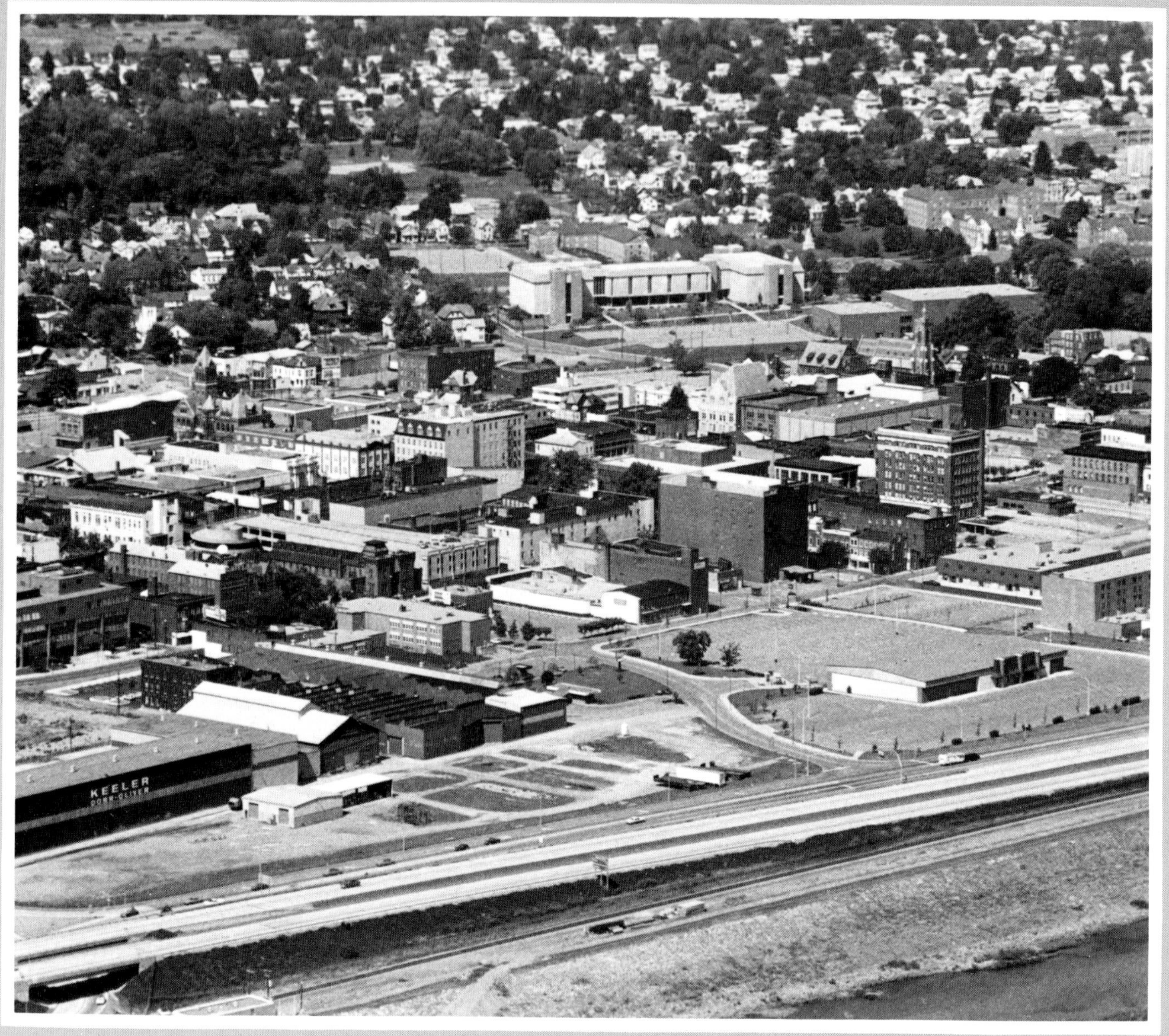
KEELER

CHAPTER SEVEN

Regional Center

Left: *This aerial view of downtown Williamsport was taken on a late summer afternoon in 1983. The Canal Street area with its new Sheraton Motor Inn is at lower right. The Genetti Lycoming Hotel is at left center. The Academic Center and new gymnasium of Lycoming College dominate the right center part of the picture. Courtesy, Marlin D. Fausey and Michael G. Roskin*

Williamsport and Lycoming County are the regional centers of North-Central Pennsylvania. In one sense this has been true since their establishment, when the county comprised the entire north-central region of the state and the city served as its county seat. In the mid-19th century the rise of the lumber industry made the community the economic hub of the region as well. In another sense the role of the city and county as regional centers has developed since World War II when they became much more complete centers of social and economic life. Law and business continue to be important, but in recent years the city and county have become regional centers of education, health care, and the arts as well.

These developments occurred during a period of significant population changes. Between 1950 and 1980 the county grew from 101,249 to 118,416 residents. This represented a 17 percent growth rate, slightly more than the 13 percent rate the state experienced during the same period. Williamsport has not been so fortunate and suffered a dramatic population decline in the same period, a loss of 26 percent since 1950. The most recent census counted 33,401 inhabitants, down 4,517 or 11.9 percent since 1970. In fact, every Pennsylvania city but one lost population between 1970 and 1980. Many cities roughly comparable to Williamsport, like Wilkes-Barre, Altoona, and Johnstown, lost population at about the same rate. Such population exchanges between cities and their surrounding areas have been common in post-World War II America and have at least two clear causes: suburbanization and urban development.

The movement of people to the suburbs in search of space, lower taxes, or what they believed to be better living conditions began in the mid-1940s. By 1960 the city had lost significant numbers of citizens to the nearby areas of Loyalsock Township, Montoursville, Old Lycoming Township, and Woodward Township. Loyalsock Township grew so rapidly that it built its own junior-senior high school in 1956. All these suburbs have continued to grow since 1960, but the rate of growth has moderated except in the areas to the west of the city. New residents, drawn by available land, the new Industrial Park, and the new Williamsport Area High School, have continued to

Above: *By the 1970s housing construction had filled up most of the level areas of Loyalsock Township and was beginning to advance up the hills. Valley View Associates were in the process of building their apartment complex north of Four Mile Drive in the fall of 1971. Courtesy, Vannucci Foto*

pour into Woodward and Old Lycoming townships at substantial rates.

As suburbanization slowed in the 1960s, urban redevelopment and renewal picked up. Programs like the West Edwin Street Renewal Project involved the demolition of old structures and the construction of high-rise apartments. The West Edwin Street Project evolved into a series of renewal efforts, like the Homesteading Program, which offered low interest loans to save older homes by rehabilitation. Other efforts, like the Canal Street Urban Renewal project, resulted in substantial loss of housing, as homes were replaced by roads, parking lots, and businesses. People and institutions were uprooted and scattered to locations in and out of the city. The city began another renewal effort in 1981, the Main Street Project, aimed at revitalizing downtown buildings and enhancing both their appearance and commercial usefulness. These varied programs have had positive results but the city has not yet halted the exodus of its citizens.

Williamsport has been able to maintain and enhance its status as a regional center despite the loss of more than one-quarter of its population for several reasons. The city and its surrounding

Above, right: *When people were moved by urban renewal or simply decided to settle in the suburbs they often took their religious institutions with them or created new ones. Congregation Ohev Shalom moved from West Edwin Street to Cherry Street in the early 1950s.*

area has had an important resource in a large number of public spirited citizens, working as individuals or as part of small groups. These people have led, coaxed, pushed, and pulled their fellow citizens to support their visions of the future and their specific plans, like the dikes, the Keystone Shortway, and the establishment of new health care facilities. They have not always been successful. One of the ironies of the city's history since

1970 has been that areas of long-term strength, retail trade, and industry have declined.

Community leaders have united with or been joined in their efforts by formal organizations, particularly the Williamsport-Lycoming Chamber of Commerce and its predecessors, as well as one of its creations, the Industrial Properties Corporation. The area has also been blessed with financial resources large enough to launch new projects. Individual philanthropy and several private foundations have

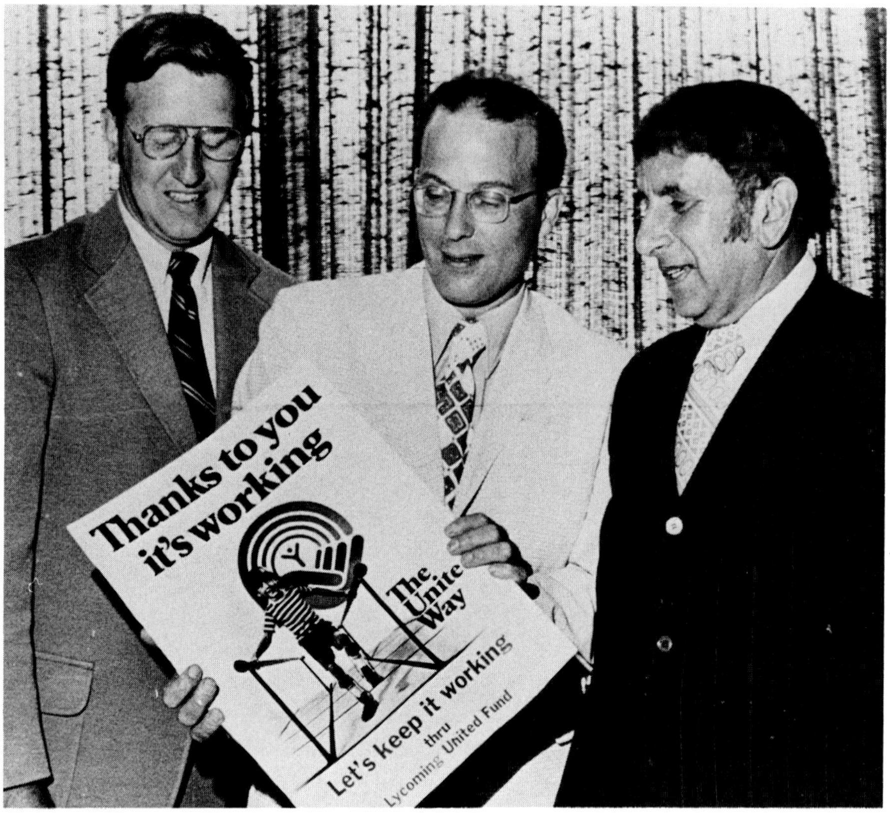

Three leaders of the 1973 Lycoming United Fund are pictured here discussing goals. From left to right are Peyton D. McDonald, corporate division leader, Harold D. Hershberger, Jr., drive leader, and William Pickelner, assistant campaign chairman. The Fund passed its goal in October and raised $691,000 for community projects. Courtesy, Grit Publishing Company

been joined by one public agency, the Williamsport Foundation or Community Trust, and have poured many millions of dollars, from seed money to capital funds, into a great variety of efforts to enhance community life. The Foundation was created in 1916 with assets of $31, and is one of the 10 oldest community foundations in America. Since 1930 it has given $10.5 million to a variety of community causes, including $500,000 to Lycoming College for its Academic Center, $500,000 to Williamsport Hospital for Capital Funds, $300,000 to Hope Enterprises for its Rehabilitation Workshop, and $200,000 for the Center City Mall project. The Foundation's assets totaled $15 million in 1983.

If public-spirited citizens with vision are the key to the city's recent development, controling the Susquehanna River stands as

Above: *Although P.D. (Percy David) Mitchell was born in Virginia and educated in North Carolina, he gave his lifetime of community service to Williamsport. He came to the city in 1943 as director of the Bethune-Douglass Community Center. When he retired in 1976 he had touched and improved the lives of countless Williamsporters. In 1976 he was governor of Kiwanis in Pennsylvania. He received many honors, including a doctorate from Lycoming College in 1969 and the Grit Award for Meritorious Community Service in 1976. He died in 1981. Courtesy, Vannucci Foto*

Right: *Williamsport has attracted candidates for national political office. Lyndon Johnson visited in 1960 as the Democratic candidate for vice president and Jimmy Carter was in town in 1976 as the Democratic presidential candidate. Carter greeted people and spoke at the bandshell in Brandon Park. Courtesy, Michael G. Roskin*

their single most important success. Williamsport and its cross-river neighbor, South Williamsport, have grown and prospered at the discretion of the river. The thunderous sounds of the ice breaking up in the spring have not always been welcomed, for the spring thaws have often meant water in the streets, houses in the river, and the interruption of all transportation and business. Then in 1955, the dikes, aided by flood control dams on the watershed, tamed the mighty Susquehanna. The idea to use dikes had been raised over the years, but not until the disastrous 1936 flood were many people convinced that dikes were the only adequate answer. Attorney John C. Youngman, Sr., chaired the Flood Control Committee of the Community Trade Association, a predecessor of the

Left: *If the 1936 flood persuaded residents to vote for the dikes, the 1946 flood reminded them how much they were needed. Lycoming Creek rose higher in 1946 than in 1936. It undermined the piers of the West Fourth Street Bridge and dropped the north side of the bridge six feet.* Courtesy, Grit Publishing Company

Williamsport-Lycoming Chamber of Commerce. His efforts reached a climax in April 1940, when the citizens of the city and South Williamsport voted for the dikes. Ground was broken in November of that year on the banks of Lycoming Creek near West Fourth Street, but war brought the project to a halt. Construction resumed in 1946 and took nine years and $15,250,000 to complete.

The wisdom of building the dikes became evident to every person living in Williamsport in June 1972, when Hurricane

Right: *Most city residents have never seen the interior of the Hepburn Street Pumping Station although it is a vital part of the flood control system. Superintendent of the City Flood Control System, Otto R. Mueller, is holding a clipboard and talking to Mary Stull, secretary of Williamsport Civil Defense, Councilman Chester D. Wolfe, and Paul W. Reeder, director of Williamsport Civil Defense, in March 1957.* Courtesy, Grit Publishing Company

Left: *An early stage of dike construction in February 1947 shows stone and gravel fill pushed into the Susquehanna River channel to form a base for the dike. This view is west from the Market Street Bridge. The Reading Railroad Station is visible on the right.* Courtesy, Grit Publishing Company

Agnes struck the area. Rainfall on June 22 was a record 8.66 inches and the subsequent river crest reached a record 34.75 feet, yet downtown Williamsport remained free of water and served (in the unusual flood-time role) as the center of help for others. Some of those needing help lived in the typically flood-free northern parts of the city where entrances to conduits carrying streams under the city clogged. Grafius Run, for example, poured over Elmira and adjacent streets.

Up and down the river areas unprotected by dikes suffered heavy damage and whole sections of the county floodplain communities of Jersey Shore, Muncy, and Montgomery were

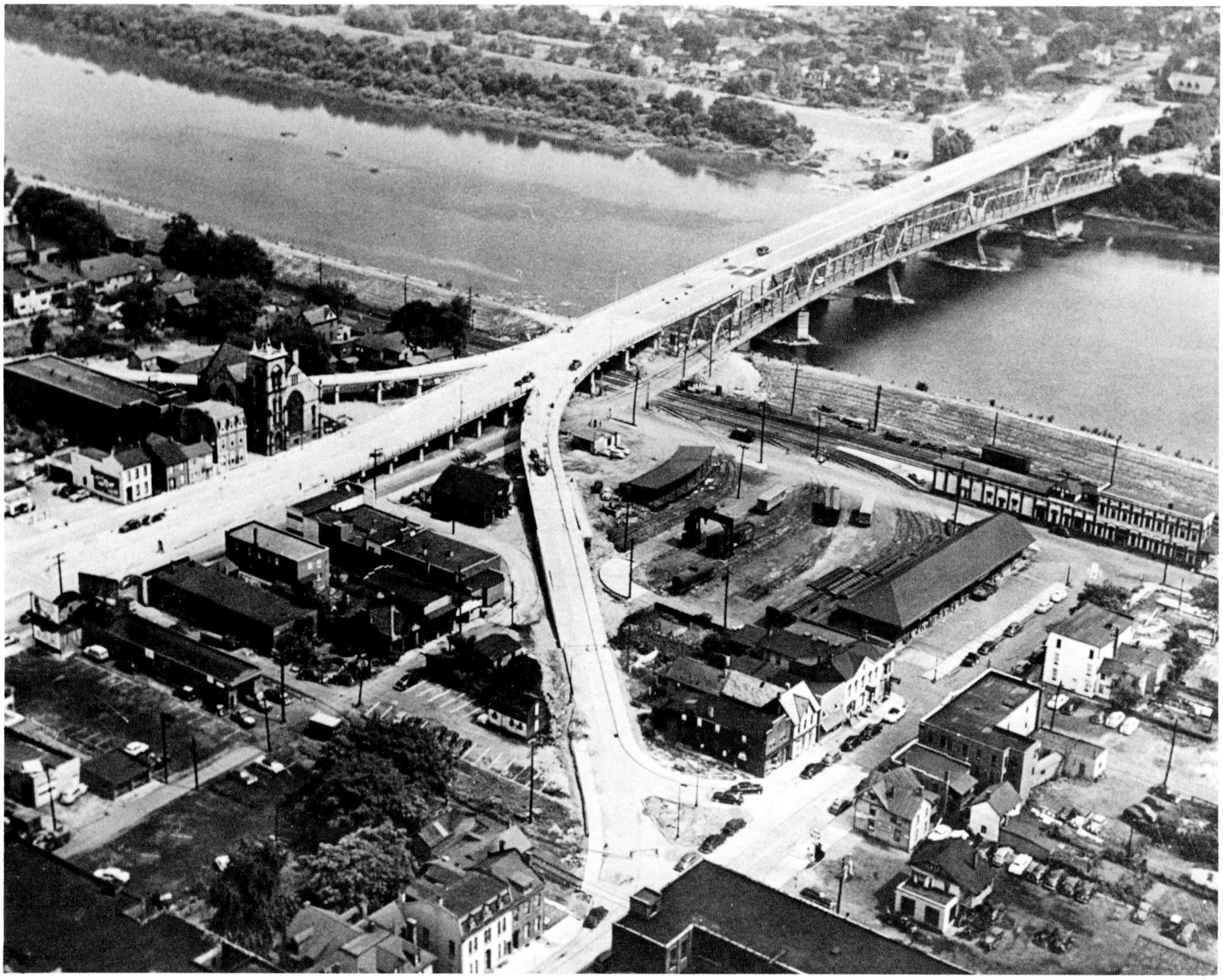

inundated. Agnes has been described as the greatest natural disaster in the history of Lycoming County, but it would have been immensely more destructive if the dikes had not kept the water away from the city.

The dikes promised Williamsport a future different from its past. They ended the cycles of destruction and reconstruction. They have not been, however, the only recent shaper of the city's life. Williamsporters have always been concerned with their routes to the world, from use of the river, to the development of the West Branch Canal, to the completion of very extensive railroad lines. As recently as 1940 the railroads' passenger and freight services seemed adequate for any future economic development. Perhaps no one projected then that within 40 years the passenger stations would have disappeared and the long freight docks would have been replaced by streets and

Left: *The old and new Market Street bridges stand side by side in August 1951, shortly before the new one opened and the old one was removed. The new bridge was much wider and met the demands of the vastly increased postwar use of private transportation. Courtesy, Grit Publishing Company*

housing projects. The last passenger train left the city on April 30, 1971. Long before this departure people with vision had worked to guarantee that the city and Lycoming County would be served by the most modern routes to the world: super highways.

The most important of these super highways is Interstate 80, providing Williamsport with easy, rapid access to points east and west. The manager of the Community Trade Association,

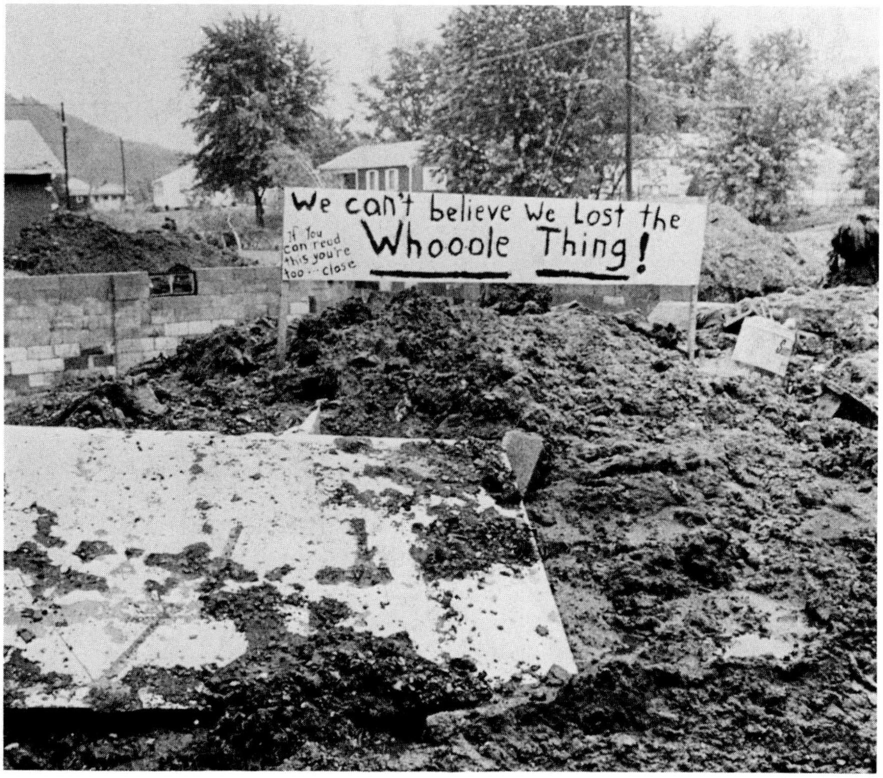

Right: *Hurricane Agnes swept the Kenyon Avenue home of George Lepley from its foundation and deposited it, twisted and broken, two blocks away. Lepley not only retained his sense of humor but also vowed to rebuild on the same site. Courtesy, Grit Publishing Company*

Charles E. Noyes, developed the idea for a Short Route to the 1939 New York World's Fair which directed travelers from Cleveland to New York City by way of Williamsport. The route proved popular and led to a plan, developed in 1952, for a toll road cutting across the northern tier of Pennsylvania, on the model of the Pennsylvania Turnpike which crosses the southern part of the state. Two years later an editor of the *Grit* Kenneth D. Rhone, coined the name, "Shortway", and in December 1954 the Keystone Shortway Association was organized. Williamsport businessman Z.H. Confair, later the state senator from Williamsport, served as president, and Noyes as executive director. This association built public and political support for the highway, which gradually changed in both location and designation. The planned road was moved from the northern tier to just south of Williamsport and from a toll road to a part of the Interstate System. On May 31, 1958, Governor George M. Leader broke ground for the new super highway in East Stroudsburg. Completed in 1970, the Keystone Shortway became a link in a major transcontinental route from New York City to San Francisco and an important element in Williamsport life. In the following decade the Susquehanna Beltway, designated Interstate 180, connected the river cities in Lycoming County with the Shortway. Williamsport has always been on the nation's roadmaps and it continues to have a favorable location on the most modern highways.

The regional status of Williamsport and Lycoming County since World War II has depended not only on the physical changes brought about by the dikes and highways, but also on developments in a variety of social and economic areas of life. The two areas of traditional strength have been law and business.

The legal system has grown in Williamsport with the expansion of court facilities and important changes in the county and federal judiciaries. Both county and federal governments built new homes in the 1970s. The Lycoming County Court House was built in 1971, and the United States Government erected a Federal Building in 1977. Opponents of these projects, led by the Williamsport Community Arts Council and the Lycoming County Historical Society, did not deny the need for new offices but argued for the preservation of historically important and artistically attractive structures. They failed to save the old courthouse but succeeded in preserving the old federal building, now remodeled and in use as city hall. The new buildings stand two blocks apart on West Third Street, and together testify to the important role of law in the area. The new courthouse has three courtrooms where there were once two, and since 1981 three judges where there were formerly two. The Federal Building, named the Herman T. Schneebeli Office Building in honor of Congressman Schneebeli, has new court facilities. Judge Malcolm Muir, judge of the United States District Court for the Middle District of Pennsylvania, has sat in Williamsport since the District Office opened in 1970, but he shared his time with Lewisburg until the construction of the new building. The new court space and expanded judicial services have played a significant role in the substantial increase in local and federal legal activity in the city.

The other area of traditional strength, business, has had troubled times. City retail trade has suffered from suburbanization and an apparent lack of vision and planning on the part of business and community leaders. As people moved to the suburbs some retail businesses followed them, setting up in shopping centers and malls. The malls began in the 1960s and multiplied in the 1970s to the point of threatening the very survival of downtown retail trade. Those east of the city have been particularly strong and vigorous, including Loyalsock Township's Loyal Plaza on its "Golden Strip" and Hall Station's Crown American's Lycoming Mall. The city lost W.T. Grant company to Loyal Plaza in 1971 and Sears, Roebuck, and Company to Lycoming Mall in 1978. In addition, a number of old downtown businesses closed, including Prior and Salada Company (1896) and the Carroll House (1929). The Grower's Market shut down in 1974 and Market Street became strangely silent for the first time since the earliest days of the city.

Dedication ceremonies for the new Federal Building were held in April 1978. The building was plagued by construction delays. Former Congressman Schneebeli jokingly accepted some responsibility for them, saying that the builders had to redesign the front to accommodate his long name. Schneebeli was flanked by federal and local officials, including Congressman Allen Ertel, seated third from the left, and Mayor Daniel P. Kirby, seated third from the right. Courtesy, Grit Publishing Company

By the mid-1970s city retailers and political leaders had organized and had begun to fight hard to stem the outward flow with a variety of promotions and projects. One of them, the Center City Mall, dedicated in November 1976, created an improved and attractive downtown setting. The project turned Pine Street into a mall, planted trees throughout the downtown area, and renewed enthusiasm for the city's retail business life, but the future seems to promise a continued struggle for downtown retailers. What the city lost, the county gained and more, so that the area continues to be a regional retail center.

The industrial life of the city has also changed since 1945 but not as dramatically as retail trade. Many of the city's largest industries, like Avco and Bethlehem Steel, which had immersed themselves in war production, successfully returned to civilian work, but with much reduced labor forces. Other industries were

more war-related, like the Susquehanna Ordnance Depot. Although located outside the city, it employed a substantial number of city residents.

The postwar loss of jobs and some industries created a crisis that was met, in part, by the Industrial Properties Corporation, which developed an industrial park in 1956 on land on Reach Road in the west end of the city. The project began slowly with one tenant, the Steelex Corporation. During the years it attracted a number of industries which offered a new diversity in employment and production, and by 1984 it included 300 acres occupied by 30 industries which employed approximately 3,000 people.

Industrial growth has also taken place elsewhere in Lycoming County, particularly in the communities of Muncy and Jersey Shore, where industrial parks have been established since 1970. But industrial change and growth have not fully kept pace with population growth. Since the mid-1970s high unemployment, often more than 10 percent and above both the state and national averages, has plagued the area and demonstrated the need for new efforts to attract more industry. Such efforts have been initiated in recent years under the leadership of the

Left: *The interior of Alcan Cable Company is pictured here at its large facility in the Industrial Park in 1967. Miles and miles of cable await processing. Courtesy, Grit Publishing Company*

Williamsport-Lycoming Chamber of Commerce.

Education, health care, and the arts have joined law and business as important aspects of Williamsport life in the years since World War II. Change has taken place in all areas of learning, including public, private, higher, and special education. Public education has undergone massive reorganization, mandated by state legislation. The 1947 education act required jointures of schools in small boroughs and townships and the education legislation of 1961 ordered unification of jointures into larger school districts. In 1940 the county had almost 100 one-room schools. When Rose Valley and Beech Valley schools closed in 1967 it had none. In exchange for such centralization and the extensive busing of students, the students have broader curriculums, larger social environments, and more extensive extra-curricular activities.

From an administrative viewpoint, local control of education passed into the hands of eight school districts, the largest of which is the Williamsport Area School District. It has experimented with innovative educational settings, like the open school, and has remodeled or built many buildings, including a large high school. The high school, proposed in 1967, spawned one of the major political controversies of the postwar era. A taxpayers group, the Citizens Responsibility Committee, filed a lawsuit challenging the school board on the cost of the proposed school and the procedures used in acquiring the land. Judge Thomas Wood ruled for the school board and the taxpayers appealed, delaying construction. The school finally opened in January 1972.

Private education has existed alongside public education for many years in Williamsport, but it has flourished since 1968. The Roman Catholics opened St. Ann's, an elementary school, in Loyalsock Township that year and consolidated St. Joseph's and St. Mary's high schools into Bishop Neumann the following year. Protestant "Christian" schools have emerged, and two of them, the Williamsport Christian Schools of Emmanuel Baptist Church, which began in 1971, and Faith Tabernacle Christian Academy, organized in 1974, offer classes from kindergarten through high school. The West Branch School, the only non-religious private school in the area, opened in 1971 on the open school model, featuring independent study and a neighborhood school atmosphere with much parent involvement.

The truly dramatic growth in education has been at the college level. At the end of World War II Williamsport had one small liberal arts institution, Dickinson Junior College, enrolling

Left: *Students at the School of Hope presented Dr. and Mrs. Max C. Miller, who had been instrumental in founding the school, with a special Christmas decoration they created in 1967. The decoration, a partridge in a pear tree, was erected in the yard of the Miller home. Courtesy, Grit Publishing Company*

Right: *The Williamsport Area High School sits atop a ridge in the northwestern end of the city. Completed in 1972, at a cost of $15.6 million, it covers 9.87 acres and features a 1,600-seat auditorium, a large gymnasium and swimming pool, and a 6,000-seat stadium. Courtesy, Marlin D. Fausey and Michael G. Roskin*

about 230 students. In 1984 it boasted a four-year liberal arts school, Lycoming College, with 1,200 students, a two-year liberal arts, vocational and technical school, Williamsport Area Community College, with 3,675 students, and a School of Commerce with more than 100 students. Dickinson's transformation took place in 1947 under the able leadership of John W. Long, who had served as president of the junior college since 1921 and continued to lead the new college until 1955. Between 1948 and 1968, Lycoming built many new facilities, including a student center, eight new dormitories, and a new academic center, which featured a new library, a theater, a planetarium, a computer center, and a large auditorium. With a long tradition in the liberal arts and business, it has recently added computer science, mass communication, and nursing to its curriculum.

Williamsport Area Community College also grew out of an existing institution, the Williamsport Technical Institute. The Williamsport School Board created WTI in 1941 as a technical school separate from but related to its high school in order to provide technical training to high school and some post-high

school students. The Watsontown Plan, so named because it introduced Watsontown High School students into WTI's programs, began in 1945. Students from other community high schools soon followed. In 1965 the Pennsylvania Board of Education approved the transformation of the Technical Institute into a Community College and the new school opened in September of that year. Its first president, Kenneth E. Carl, had served as the last director of WTI. The college occupied the Technical Institute facilities in its early years. It expanded into the old Williamsport High School after the city vacated it. In the late 1970s, it embarked on an ambitious building program, which has thus far included new labs for its technical programs, a new library, and an Earth Science Center. It continues to offer a technical program to high school students from a number of surrounding school districts and runs an extensive adult evening education program, which enrolls about 4,500 students a year.

Education for children and adults with special disabilities has taken a great leap forward in Williamsport since the 1950s. Much of this has been mandated by state laws guaranteeing an education to all Pennsylvania citizens and has been facilitated by the creation of Intermediate Units. The one serving Williamsport and Lycoming County is Unit 17. The city, however, has had its own unique special education school since 1954, when the Lycoming Chapter of the Pennsylvania Association for Retarded Children founded the School of Hope to provide a school opportunity for children who could not attend public schools. The school merged with Enterprises for the Handicapped in 1974 to become Hope Enterprises, Inc. Hope runs several programs, including the school, renamed the Dr. Max C. Miller Training Center in 1981, and the Rehabilitation Workshop.

Health care has matched education in growth and development and has made Williamsport an important medical center. Williamsport Hospital grew dramatically in the decades after 1950 under the leadership of Daniel W. Hartman, Harry R. Gibson, and Clive R. Waxman. Beginning with a new V-shaped addition to the southern side of its main building in 1952, the hospital built a new home for its School of Nursing, a Rehabilitation Center, a Medical Center, and most recently a Core Services Building in 1974. Its major diagnostic tools include a CAT Scan and a Sonography Unit. It has established a variety of educational programs and continues to run "the oldest functioning nursing school in Pennsylvania."

Williamsport Hospital was the only medical facility in the city until 1951, when it was joined by Divine Providence Hospital. Mary Hills grew up in the city and became Mother Theresilla of the Sisters of Christian Charity. She dreamed of opening a home for the elderly in the city. The Sisters, with the help of Father Leo J. Post, pastor of St. Boniface Church, bought land in the northeastern corner of the city, raised funds, and built a hospital as their version of this dream. It no sooner opened its doors than it began to grow, adding a chapel, an auditorium, a convent, and in 1975 an East Wing, which contains emergency services and many of its special centers, including the region's Hemodialysis and Cancer Treatment centers. The Community Mental Health Center for Lycoming-Clinton Counties also makes its home in this medical complex. Williamsport and Divine Providence hospitals have many complimentary services which together have lifted Williamsport's medical care to regional status.

The arts have joined education and health care in their attainments. Williamsport has a remarkable tradition in the fields of music and theater. It boasts the oldest continuing band in the United States, the Repasz-Elks Band, as well as the Imperial Teteques, reborn in 1963 and named for the Williamsport Imperial Teteques, "the original all-Masonic music organization in the U.S." The Williamsport Symphony

Right: *Dogwoods in bloom in Brandon Park create a wonderful sense of beauty for visitors.*

Right: *The campus of Lycoming College features a quadrangle surrounded by the Wertz Student Center, the Long Administration Building, the Clarke Building and Chapel, and dormitories. The large structure in the center foreground is the Academic Center, which was completed in 1968. The Athletic Stadium and fields are several blocks north of the main campus. Courtesy, Marlin D. Fausey and Michael G. Roskin*

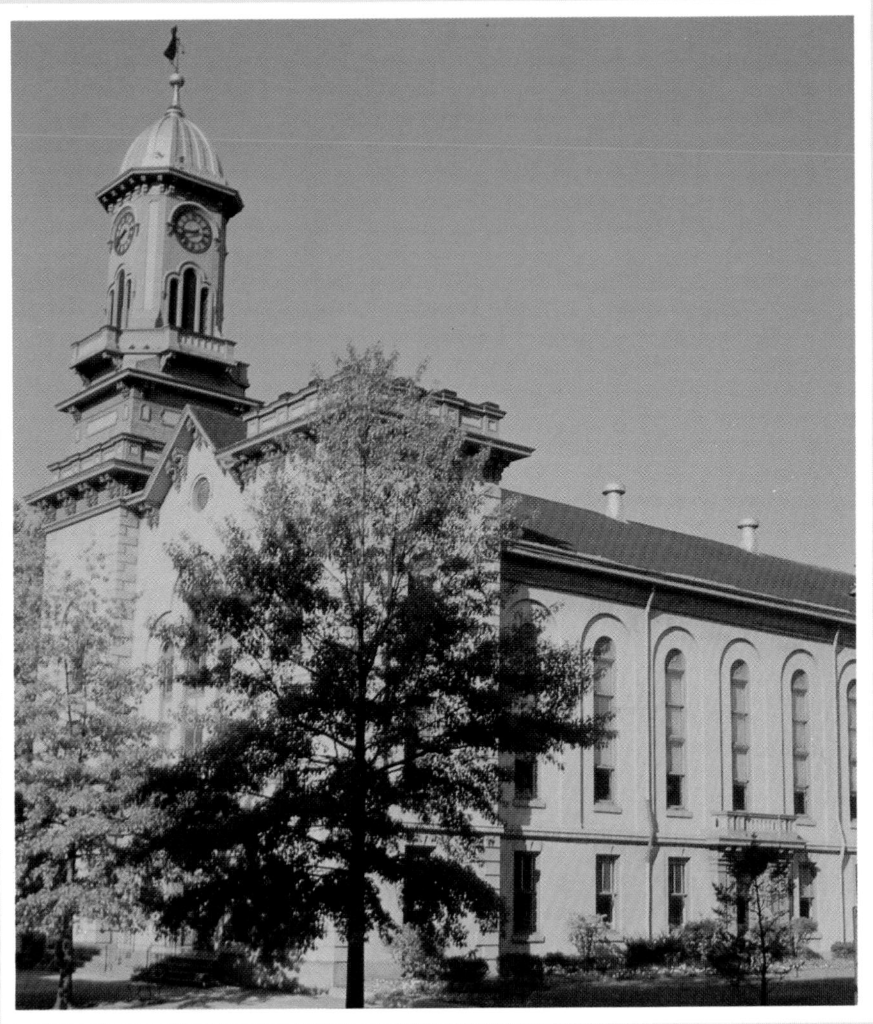

Left: *This courthouse served Lycoming County from 1860 until 1969. Designed by the well-known Pennsylvania architect Samuel Sloan, its stately form lives on in similarly designed courthouses in the nearby towns of Sunbury and Lock Haven. Courtesy, Ralph E. Menne*

Right: *Peter Herdic paid for the construction of this English Gothic church and then gave it to Trinity Episcopal Parish in 1876 for the sum of one dollar with the stipulation that the pews were to remain "forever free." It is built of Bald Eagle Mountain stone. Judge John Maynard presented the church with Westminster Chimes, the first church in the United States to have them.*

Left: *The current Lycoming County Court House is the third to occupy the traditional court site of Pine and West Third streets. Built at the cost of $3.5 million, it brought an expanding county government under one roof. County offices began to move in during December 1970, but official dedication ceremonies were not until May 1971. Courtesy, Ralph E. Menne*

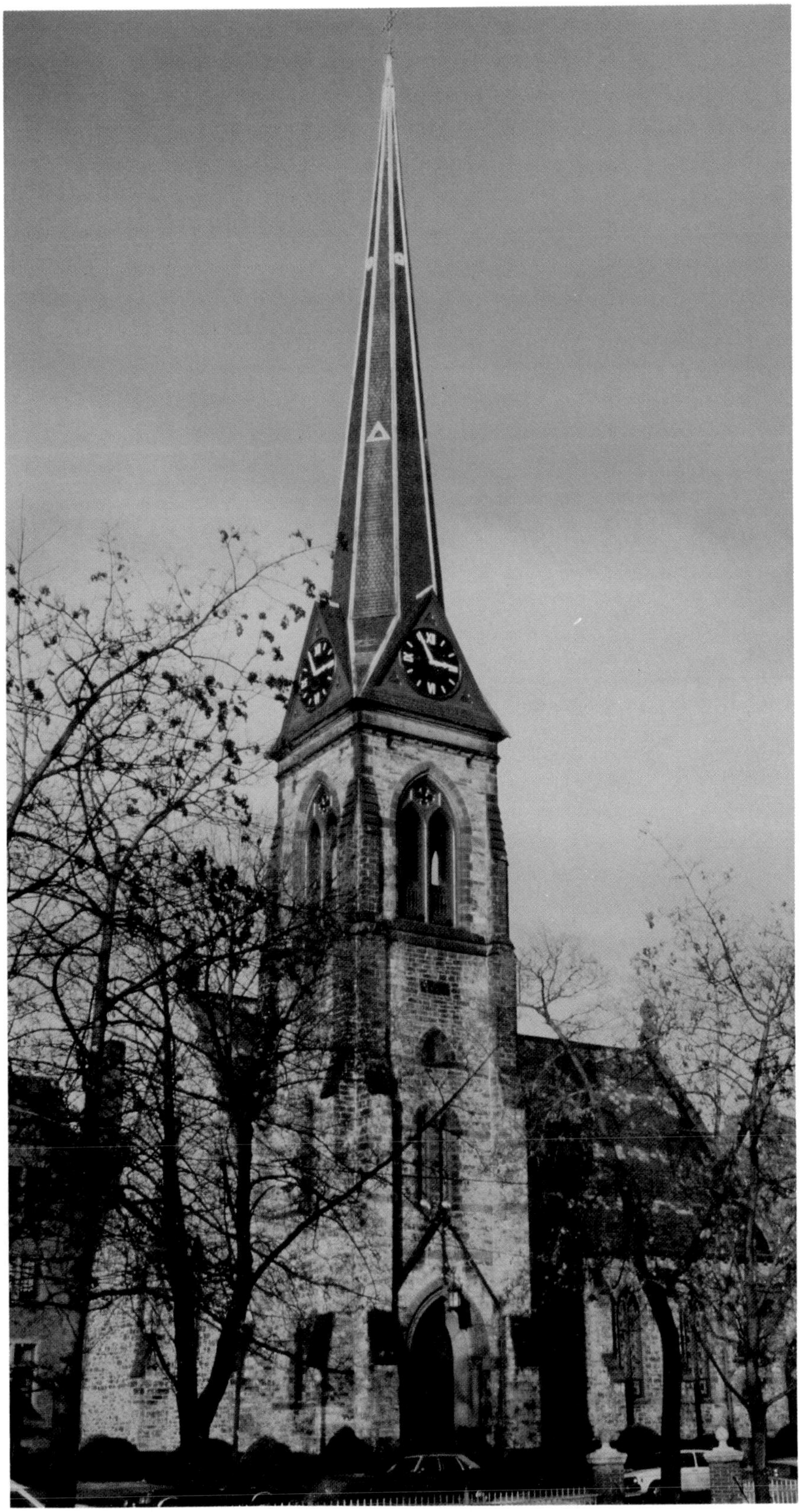

Right: *Several prominent Williamsport families have owned the Emery House on West Fourth Street since it was built in 1889 by William Emery as a wedding present for his bride, Mary White Gamble. Although it has become an office building, its Romanesque style has been carefully maintained as has its stained glass and woodwork.*

Below: *Cornelius Woodward moved from New Orleans to Natchez and eventually to Williamsport where in 1803 he erected a four-room log house. He subsequently enlarged the home to 19 rooms, building it to reflect a Natchez-style architecture. Named Springside in 1849 by John Vanderbelt Woodward, it remained in the Woodward family until 1945. The spacious lawn is graced by a fountain which was once part of the Peter Herdic estate and is shadowed by a great copper beech tree planted by Cornelius' wife in 1802.*

Above: *This painting is one of more than 200 such compositions Severin Roesen is known to have created. Born in Germany in about 1816, he immigrated to the United States and lived in New York City for a time. He moved to Williamsport about 1859 where he lived until he died some 13 years later. In 1979 one of his paintings brought $50,000 at a New York City auction. Courtesy, Ralph E. Menne*

Right: *The Ulman Opera House, built on Market Square in 1867, was the first opera house in Williamsport. This painting captures it in its grandeur with its mansard roof intact. Courtesy of PNC Bank.*

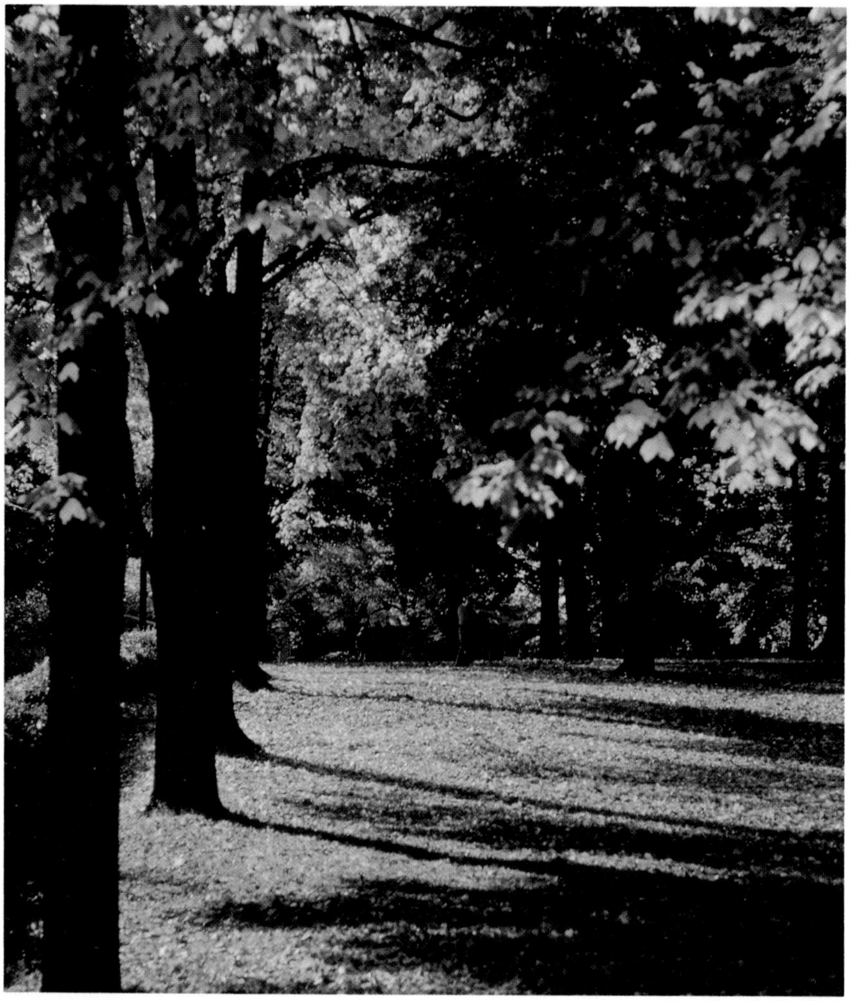

Top: *The* Hiawatha, *a project of the Williamsport-Lycoming Chamber of Commerce, made its maiden voyage in August 1982. It was named after a popular turn-of-the-century riverboat which sailed the Susquehanna between Williamsport and Sylvan Dell. Courtesy, Marlin D. Fausey*

Far left: *A corridor of fall colors and shadows graces Brandon Park. Courtesy, Michael G. Roskin*

Above: *Crowds pack the Howard J. Lamade Stadium during the Little League World Series in late August 1970. The Little League Baseball, Inc., complex is located in South Williamsport. The central part of the stadium was completed in 1959 in time for the World Series that year. The first and third base extensions were added in 1968. Courtesy, Ralph E. Menne*

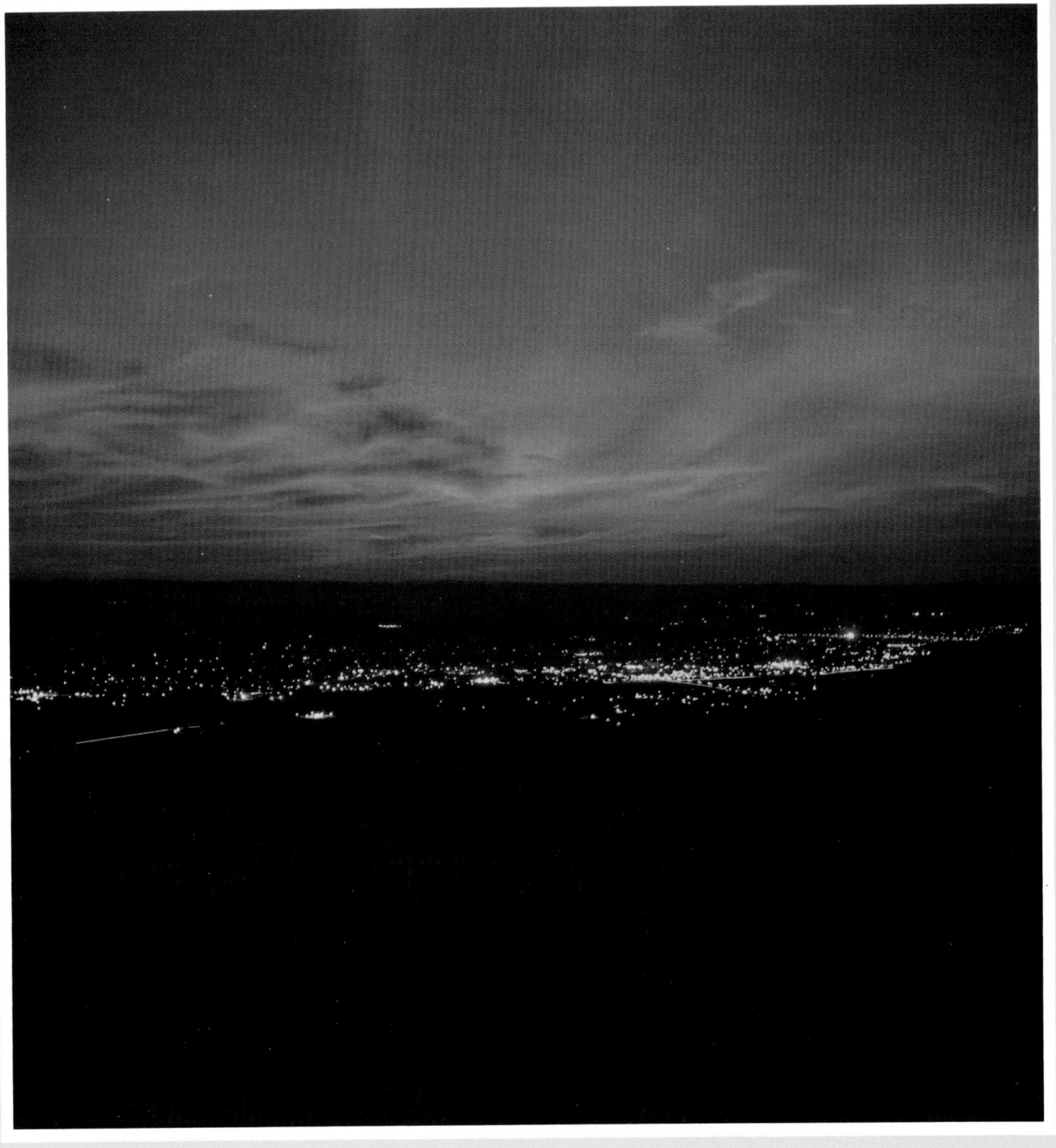

Left: *Williamsport is seen at sunset from Bald Eagle Mountain. The city stretches for miles along the Susquehanna River and gives the impression of a large metropolitan area. Courtesy, Ralph E. Menne*

Orchestra, with Osborne Housel as conductor, played concerts for a 10-year span after its creation in 1948. The Susquehanna Valley Orchestra, formed in 1966, became a regional orchestra with Williamsport as one of its two concerts centers. In 1984 it was renamed the Williamsport Symphony Orchestra, the city serving as home base. Choral groups have added their voices to the music of the city. The oldest of these is the Gesang Verein Harmonia, founded by John Fischer in 1892. Thomas H. Shellenberger became director in 1975. Choral music in the city has been shaped since 1944 in large measure by Walter G. McIver. In that year he founded the Civic Choir, later the Civic Chorus. Two years later, as a faculty member of Lycoming College, he formed the Lycoming College Choir. The Civic Choir has had a distinguished life under McIver and his successors, Jay Stenger and Paul Ziegler, and has given many memorable performances, including *The Messiah* in 1948 and 1949, and *Amahl and the Night Visitors* in 1952 and 1953.

Theater, like music, has a distinguished history. In the 19th century performances were given by companies of traveling professional actors and singers at such places as the Ulman Opera House and the Lycoming Opera House. The theater of the mid-20th century has continued to include visiting professionals, but has been dominated by companies of local amateurs. The local groups include the Williamsport Players, organized in 1958, the Drama Workshop, founded in 1969, and the Community Theater League, created in 1976. Lycoming College's Arena Theater has offered summer as well as academic year dramatic productions since 1962. The city also has a Civic Ballet Company.

The arts are more than music and theater. Artists and craftsmen have created a wide variety of groups, including the Williamsport Chapter of the Pennsylvania Guild of Craftsmen in 1949, the Williamsport Creative Writers Forum in 1959, and the Bald Eagle Art League in 1972. Local artist Horace Hand, known for his Christmas Eve Church paintings published by the Williamsport *Sun-Gazette,* presided over the league until his death in 1977.

The arts have flourished because of local talent and widespread community support. They have been assisted by the Williamsport Community Arts Council, an organization proposed by the Williamsport Chamber of Commerce and carried out by Barnard Taylor and others. Its Festival of the Arts in 1960 has been followed by a variety of shows and performances, including a month-long festival in 1971. The October Festival of Arts, begun in 1973, has been the united effort of the Arts Council and the Art Department of the Williamsport Area School District, under the direction of June E. Baskin. Public celebrations in Williamsport invariably include the arts, further testimony to their importance in the life of the city.

Williamsport and Lycoming County have not only maintained their status as regional centers since 1945, but have enhanced it with significant developments in education, music, and the arts. Greater achievement in quality and quantity are doubtless attainable in every life area. City and county leaders have continued, for example, to be concerned with industrial growth and the survival of city retail trade. But even as these concerns exist, many of the same people have projected a new area of growth for the 1980s: recreation and tourism.

Williamsport has an impressive recreational tradition. Before the completion of the beltway, anyone who tried to travel near or in the city at the start of trout season in the spring, or buck season in the fall, faced incredible traffic congestion and learned the hard way that they were at the crossroads of a major sporting area. The city also had professional baseball teams for many of the years from 1940-1976, and a professional basketball team, the Williamsport Billies, from 1947-1964. These regional professional leagues were joined by Little League baseball beginning in 1939.

Carl E. Stotz was the founder and moving spirit of Little League. The first Little League World Series was held at Memorial Park in 1947. Little League has grown from 28 teams in seven leagues in Pennsylvania in 1946 to approximately 48,500 teams in about 6,900 leagues in many countries of the world in 1983. Every August the Williamsport area is the center of national sports attention as national television and tens of thousands of visitors come for the championship game.

While Little League has been and continues to be very important to the recreational and tourist life of the Williamsport area, it has not been able to lift it to the status of a regional recreation center. Community leaders have searched for additional recreational resources and believe they have found them in the Susquehanna River. The river has a long history of recreational use but in many ways it has disappeared from view for more than a generation. Canoe clubs, boat docks, and swimming beaches, once numerous, have declined dramatically. The dikes have kept the river in its channel but have also kept the people away. Indeed, until the completion of the beltway which elevated the roadbed the river was visible to city residents only from a bridge or a nearby hill. The plans of

Above: *Carl E. Stotz points to a baseball as his two nephews, Harold "Major" Gehron and Jimmy Gehron for whom he "invented" the game, listen. In the summer of 1938 Stotz experimented with a scaled-down baseball field suitable for young boys. The first Little League baseball game was played on a sandlot in Memorial Park outside the Bowman Field fence on June 6, 1939. Courtesy, Carl E. Stotz*

Below: *Susquehanna State Park is pictured in the mid-1960s before Hurricane Agnes virtually destroyed it. The park had been substantially refurbished in the early 1980s and has become home port for the riverboat,* Hiawatha. *Courtesy, Grit Publishing Company*

Right: *The new Hepburn Street Dam was under construction between 1983 and 1984. The project was funded by the Commonwealth of Pennsylvania.*

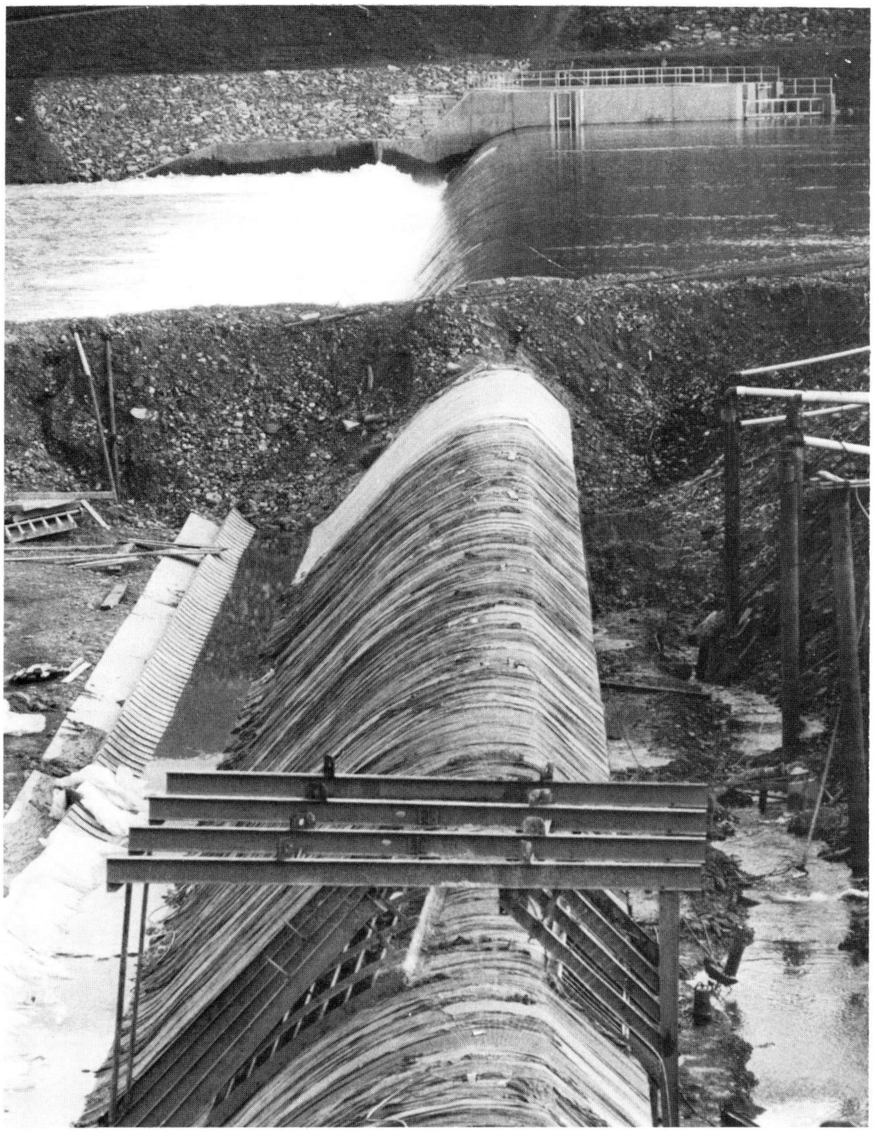

community leaders for the river have resulted in a new and stronger Hepburn Street Dam to guarantee a more stable and deeper pool upstream, the removal of the log boom cribs to open more of the "Long Reach" to boating, the construction of a new riverboat, the *Hiawatha,* to encourage use of the river and tourism, and the development of Susquehanna Park. The Susquehanna Boom Festival, begun by the Williamsport Jaycees in 1981, has highlighted the roles of lumber and the river in the area's life.

Michael Ross' early survey, the development of the canal and railroads, the building of the lumber boom, the development of a diversified industrial base at the turn of the century, and the building of the dikes and Shortway have brought a degree of growth and prosperity to Williamsport that is rare in the Appalachian region. This growth was made possible by the vigor, determination, and vision of its citizens. Today, Williamsport is at a crossroads. It is facing the decline of its retail trade and relatively high unemployment in its traditional industries. But again, the community seems determined to move forward. In 1982 the city adopted the motto, "A Proud Past and a Promising Future."

LYCOMING BICENTE
1795-1995

Chapter Eight

EPILOGUE

by John F. Piper, Jr.

The Sand Sculpture depicted aspects of Lycoming County History. Sponsored by the Lycoming Mall as part of the County Bicentennial. Courtesy, Lycoming County Historical Museum

More than ten years have slipped by since the initial printing of this book and nothing has happened to change its fundamental perspective about Williamsport. It remains a vital regional center, not just of Lycoming County but of an extended area reaching in all directions. This Epilogue develops the story of the years 1985 to the present, using the various themes formulated in the first edition. This account concludes with a review of some of the major features of the celebration of the Lycoming County Bicentennial in 1995, which was an effort to make the population of the region more aware of the rich heritage and continuing vitality of the county and its major city.

People, their interaction with the natural environment and with one another, form the basis of any society. The Census of 1990 indicated the county population had remained stable since 1980, but that Williamsport had lost 1,468 during those years. This decline was not new since the city, like most urban centers, had been losing population since 1950. The data signals the slowing of migration to the suburbs. The nature of suburban migration changed as well. The old suburban growth had been primarily along the floodplain in areas directly connected to the city, so that outsiders could hardly distinguish the boundaries between suburb and city. Since the late 1980's, however, suburbanites have moved up into and over the hills surrounding Williamsport. Some of these areas contain very upscale houses on large plots of land. Almost every road north of the city has at least one of these new developments, with the most dramatic ones off both sides of Poco Farm Road in Loyalsock Township. They are Poco Hills Estates to the west and The Fields to the east. Between Montoursville and the Lycoming Mall, Tules Run has grown rapidly since its founding in 1991. It is not difficult to imagine virtually continuous residential settlement between that borough and the Mall in the future.

The population of the city has not only declined, it has also changed. By far the most noted development has been the arrival of a new immigrant or migrant group, most of whom have been people of color, primarily African-Americans. They began to arrive in the mid 1980's at the rate of 300 to 400 a year, and they have continued to come in the early 1990's, but in less well documented numbers. They came from urban areas in Pennsylvania and New Jersey, with substantial numbers calling Philadelphia home. A study directed by Charles Haun in 1988, *In Search of the Safety Net*, argued that the first

Poco Hills Estates, one of the newest of the suburban developments, is spreading over a good portion of the north side of Grampian Hill. Courtesy, Marlin D. Fausey and Michael G. Roskin

wave of this new group was typically made up of substance abusers involved in various kinds of treatment programs. They were encouraged to move to Williamsport, often literally pushed out of their home towns, by their counselors, and directed to one or another of the sobriety houses located in and around the city. Unfortunately, no recent study of this group has been completed. It appears, however, that those who once came, and may still come because they have been pushed, have been joined by others who have been drawn to the city by the desire to live with relatives or by word of mouth encouragement that Williamsport is simply a good place to live.

Whether pushed or pulled, the "influx" as the group has been called from its earliest years, has had a mixed reception. Caring organizations, including the Bethune-Douglass Community Center and many of the traditional African-American churches, reached out with creative programs and welcoming arms. Public debate as often as not has turned on stereotypes, and the immigrants have been blamed for a whole series of problems, including an increase in drug use and

One of the newest routes to the world, the new Route 15 curves its way north. Courtesy, Marlin D. Fausey and Michael G. Roskin

abuse, crime, and disruptions in the public schools. Whatever may be the truth of these claims, it also appears to be true that many in the new group are recovered persons, and a number of others are persons who themselves were never part of the drug scene, and most are good citizens in search of a better way of life. The result of the migration has been a new social, cultural and racial diversity in the city. The people of the city and county have been working through this new social reality, but not without some stress and not yet to a clear resolution.

A more culturally diverse population which reflects the population changes in the nation has accentuated the regional leadership of Williamsport and Lycoming County. This leadership position emerged after World War II in six areas of social and economic life. They were and continue to be: the legal system; business and industry; education; health care; the arts; and recreation and tourism.

Thomas C. Raup

The legal system, particularly the court system, belongs first in this review of Williamsport's regional importance. The decision in 1795 to locate the court of the newly formed Lycoming County in Ross' town established law as a major avenue of development. The legal system that expanded dramatically from 1950 to 1985 has continued to grow. Those who could not imagine the need for a third county judge in 1981 had to adjust to a fourth one and a new courtroom in 1992. The retirement of President Judge Thomas C. Raup in 1995, after twenty-one successful years on the bench, became the occasion for one of the most spirited judicial campaigns in local memory. When Nancy L. Butts took the oath of office in January, 1996, she became the first female judge in the history of the county.

Nancy L. Butts

The retail business life of the city was in trouble in 1985 and continued to struggle until the beginning of the current decade. Since then the signs of business departures have been more than matched by those of new life in the downtown area. The *Grit* building, vacated when the *Grit* closed, has been renovated and is currently occupied by the local offices of the State Departments of Labor and Industry and Environmental Protection. Blue Shield located a substantial regional center in the Canal Street Urban Renewal area in 1989. The buildings which once housed E. Keeler Company and its successors were demolished to make way for the construction of the largest supermarket in the Williamsport area, Wegman's. The decision of this highly successful New York based supermarket chain to locate downtown has been a major economic boost. It opened in May, 1996. A number of new restaurants have opened in the past few years.

The Williamsport-Lycoming Chamber of Commerce created the New Venture Center in 1991, which now works with 19 small businesses, ranging in size from one person operations to a company with 15 employees. Most recently, the new mayor, Steven W. Cappelli, has announced a number of economic initiatives, including a new trade and transit facility in the center of town. And if Williamsport is not yet the business center it once was and wants to be again, most of what it lost has been gained by the surrounding area. Major stores in the Lowes andWal-Mart chains have opened in

Downtown Williamsport with the Canal Street Urban Renewal area in the foreground, featuring the Blue Shield building in the right center and Wegman's on the left. Courtesy, Marlin D. Fausey and Michael G. Roskin

Montoursville. The Lycoming Mall has been in a major expansion mode for several years. Sears remodeled and grew at one end of the Mall and Kaufmann's replaced Hess' in an expanded store at the other end. And in a strip along the north side of the mall Toys R Us and Sam's Club built substantial outlets.

This revival in business, in both city and county, has not been matched by industry. Many of the local industrial parks have grown since 1985, but some major businesses have not survived the decade. Bethlehem Steel, long one of the industrial lynchpins, closed its operation in 1989. The C. A. Reed manufacturing plant closed in 1993 with the loss of over 400 jobs, and several other major industries have reduced their workforces. Efforts to encourage economic development at the industrial level have continued through the Williamsport-Lycoming Chamber of Commerce, but have not shared the success in the retail field.

The Williamsport Area School District has continued to set the pace for public schools in the region in both size and variety of educational opportunities for its students. Despite a number of controversies in the past ten years, many of them over budget matters

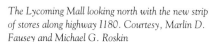

The Lycoming Mall looking north with the new strip of stores along highway I180. Courtesy, Marlin D. Fausey and Michael G. Roskin

The Lycoming College Campus, with the Heim Biology and Chemistry Building in the upper left. Courtesy, Marlin D. Fausey and Michael G. Roskin

and administrative decisions, the Williamsport schools have sustained their course.

The truly new developments in education in the region have been at the college level. It has not been part of the local culture to see Williamsport as a college town, but growth in both the colleges makes such a designation reasonable. Pennsylvania College of Technology now enrolls about 4,300 students and Lycoming College approximately 1,500. The substantial majority of these students live within the city, which means the population increases significantly for nine months every year. That means that for most of the year about one in six residents is in college.

Lycoming College began its growth with the arrival of James E. Douthat as its 14th president in 1989. Enrollments have moved from 1,200 to 1,500 in the years since. There have been a variety of physical changes on campus, including most prominently the opening of the Heim Biology and Chemistry Building in 1990, and the removal of the former science building in 1996. The college has under construction an ambitious Market to Mulberry project to provide a more direct physical connection to the downtown area.

Pennsylvania College of Technology emerged as a result of a crisis in the sponsorship of the Williamsport Area Community College. As the sponsoring agreements between the college and the local school districts neared expiration in the late 1980's, many districts indicated their desire to end their relationship with the college. The City of Williamsport stepped forward as temporary sponsor until 1989 when the college became an affiliate of The Pennsylvania State University. It has grown in many areas. Student enrollment has increased, a series of new buildings have opened, and a variety of new baccalaureate programs in technical fields have begun. The buildings include a new campus center, an advanced technology and health sciences center, a

Pennsylvania College of Technology looking south. The Bush Campus Center is in the upper left, the Breuder Technology Health Sciences Center is in the upper right, and the new dormitory construction is in the lower left. Courtesy, Marlin D. Fausey and Michael G. Roskin

professional development center, and an aviation center. The college is currently building its first dormitories, to be called The Village at Penn College, planned for occupancy in 1997.

Health services in Williamsport and the county have undergone massive transformations. Ten years ago two major facilities, the Williamsport Hospital and the Divine Providence Hospital, provided the area with excellent health care but were often in competition with one another. In 1994 they joined to create the Susquehanna Health System, with a mandate from the Office of the Attorney General of Pennsylvania to decrease their overall operating costs by $40,000,000 over a five year period. The entire process is part of the national reorganization of health care, and the question remains whether cooperation and the end of expensive competition will result in better and less expensive health care for the region.

The arts have thrived in Williamsport in the past decade. Most of the organizations and programs in place in 1985 have continued to provide many opportunities for residents in art, music, and theater. One major new development has overshadowed all others: the restoration of the former Capitol Theater and its transformation into the Community Arts Center. Robert L. Breuder, President of The Pennsylvania College of Technology, led the project. The total cost was $11,200,000, a figure that generated some controversy and stretched the financial capacity of the region. In spite of that, the fund drive raised $2,000,000 from the private sector, the largest amount ever raised for a single community project. The Center opened in 1993 and has become the jewel in the crown of the arts.

Recreation and tourism have also thrived, but not without major effort. The Williamsport-Lycoming Chamber of Commerce has continued to work hard to attract tourists to the area, and in 1987 opened the Tourist Promotion Agency (TPA) in a very attractively restored building on West Fourth Street owned by Trinity Episcopal

Church. The Herdic Trolley, a replica of an original Williamsport trolley, began to operate in 1990. The riverboat Hiawatha survived a financial crisis and continues to attract people to the Susquehanna River. Perhaps the most important recreational development in the past decade has been the return of minor league baseball to the City. The Chicago Cubs opened a farm team in 1994 and has put the city once again on the national baseball map. The new development in recreation for children and youth has been the explosive growth of youth soccer, particularly that sponsored by the American Youth Soccer Organization. It has literally taken flight from small beginnings in 1976 with less than a dozen teams to almost 200 in 1996.

The area continues to be the home of Little League Baseball. It has grown at a steady pace as a national and international organization, with operations in 81 nations. In 1989 it added a Challenger Division for mentally and physically challenged youth. At the close of 1995 there were 198,850 Little League teams with 2,982,750 participants around the world. The new symbol of its international status is a European headquarters, currently under construction in Kutnov, Poland.

A decade is a relatively short time in a two hundred year period. It

The restored interior of the Capitol Theater, now the Community Arts Center. Courtesy, Lycoming County Historical Museum

The Herdic Trolley. Courtesy, Lycoming County Historical Museum

is very difficult to discern at the moment what if anything from these most recent years will make a difference for the future. One thing seems certain and that is that the strong forward looking spirit of the people will sustain and seek to enhance the regional importance of Williamsport and Lycoming County.

The regional distinction of Williamsport and Lycoming County is based on the gathering of all the themes together and not on the strength of one or two of them. The purpose of the Lycoming County Bicentennial was to highlight as many of the aspects of the life of the area as possible. The celebration of the county's 200th birthday was also a celebration of the city.

The Board of Governors of the Lycoming County Historical Society proposed to County Commissioners Dolly M. Wilt, Paul F. Glunk, and Henry F. Frey, shortly after they were elected in 1992, that the county hold a bicentennial celebration. They agreed that the county would sponsor a celebration and appointed a Lycoming County Bicentennial Committee to develop a plan and oversee it. The Committee made its most crucial decision very early in the planning process: to focus on the rich social and economic life of the county rather than spend time and money building a monument to mark the occasion.

The Bicentennial Committee chose a logo, waves in blue and green to symbolize the river and the mountains, and created the phrase: "Celebrate the Land, the River, the People." The celebration focus from start to finish has been "the people." When the Committee began to project events it made a major discovery: the people were already involved in so many annual celebratory occasions that there was no need to create new ones. The Committee decided to select a few of the existing events and add financial resources to make it possible for the particular sponsoring groups to make them larger. The best examples of this were the Bicentennial Concert of the Williamsport Symphony Orchestra, held in April; the Bicentennial Boom Festival Parade, held in June; and the Bicentennial Art Exhibit of the Williamsport-Lycoming Arts Council, held in September and October. A *1995 Events Calendar* offered the public 52 beautiful color photographs of various sites in the city and county and listed numerous historical and contemporary events. The Committee published monthly full page ads in the *Sun-Gazette* outlining all the events already planned by individuals and groups and encouraging residents to attend them and join in the celebrations.

Although the Committee decided against a monument, it also determined to leave behind some records of life in 1995, benchmarks of the current era. It sponsored two exhibits for this purpose, with provisions to house them permanently in the Lycoming County Historical Museum. The first was the "People of Lycoming County," a review of individuals and family groups who have lived or now reside in Williamsport, and the boroughs, villages and townships of the county. Created by the Lycoming County Geneological Society, this exhibit revealed many long family lineages and exciting stories. The second exhibit was "Made in Lycoming," and highlighted the economic and business life of the area. Created under the direction of the Lycoming County Historical Society, individual panels or groups of panels of this exhibit are available for display on request.

In addition, the Bicentennial Committee worked with the Pennsylvania Historical and Museum Commission and has erected one official historical marker in the city, in honor of Carl E. Stotz the founder of Little League, and will erect two others, one to remember the life of Dietrick Lamade, the founder of the *Grit*, and the other the career of Peter Herdic, the leading lumber baron.

These exhibits demonstrate, as did the myriad events of the Bicentennial celebration, the richness of the social, cultural, and economic life of the county throughout its history and in the present day.

LYCOMING COUNTY
BICENTENNIAL
1795 - 1995

Celebrate the land the river the people

The logo of the Lycoming County Bicentennial

The Sand Sculpture depicted aspects of Lycoming County History. Sponsored by the Lycoming Mall as part of the County Bicentennial. Courtesy, Lycoming County Historical Museum

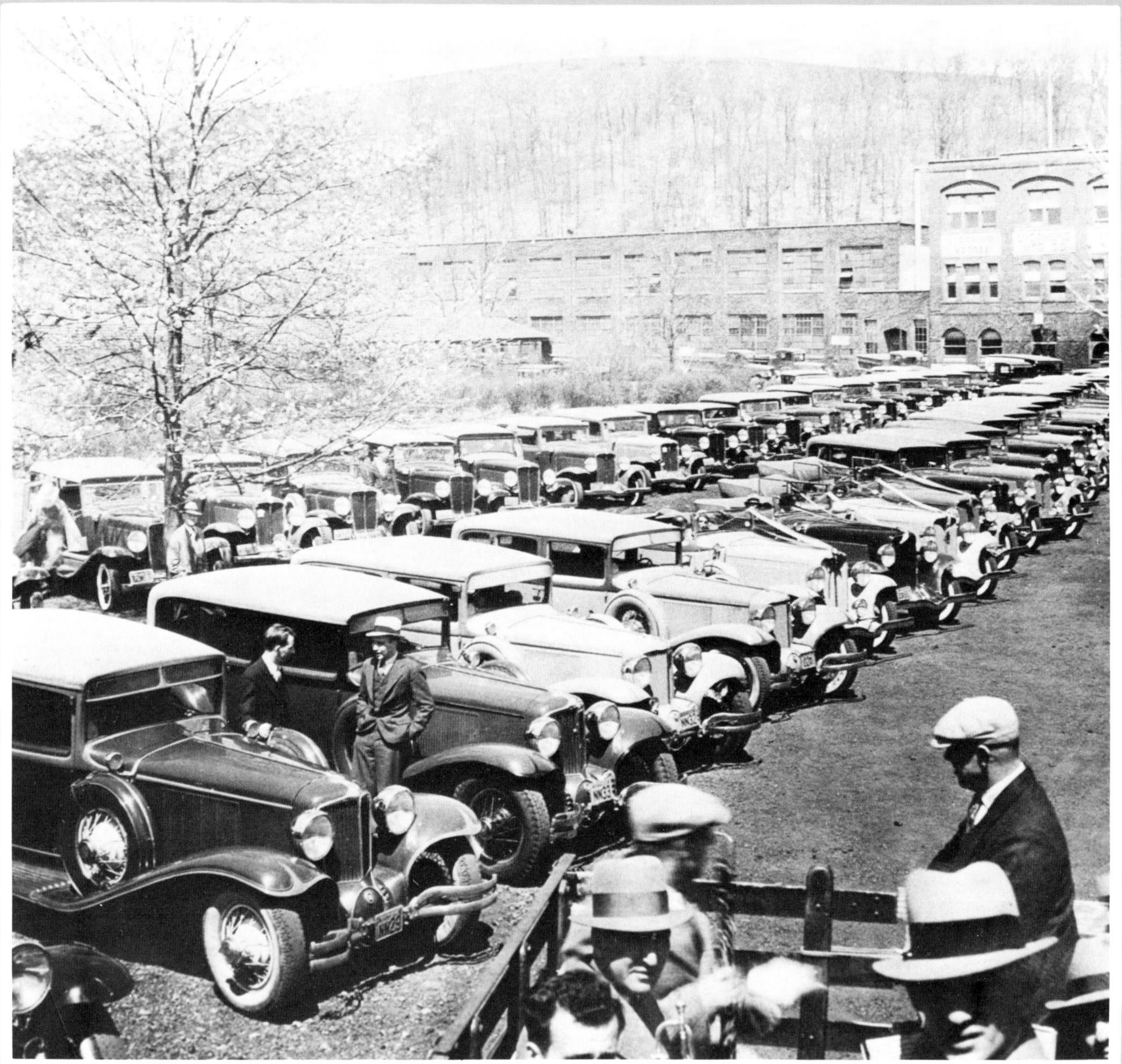

CHAPTER NINE

Partners in Progress

by Joseph P. Laver

Left: *These automobiles, among them a score of new Auburns, were part of an 80-car "boost business caravan" which toured Williamsport and South Williamsport streets in the spring of 1932. They were all powered by Lycoming Mfg. Company engines. Two airplanes, also Lycoming engine powered, flew over the city during the caravan. Courtesy, Grit Publishing Company*

The collective histories of the companies and institutions included in this chapter are a microcosm of the Williamsport area's history. Some date back to the community's initial industrialization based on lumber; some are the fruits of various organized efforts to bolster Williamsport's economic base.

Early diversification began when new businesses were spawned to meet the various needs of the lumber industry. Quite often, in order to grow, these companies would branch out into nonlumber products. Wood-related industries, from toothpicks to furniture, sprang up, which in turn generated additional firms to supply such things as machinery, parts, and packaging. And the burgeoning population kept increasing the need for services and products.

Some of these needs were met by local people starting small ventures. Others were begun by newcomers investing their personal and financial equity in a new community. Many current local businesses and industries trace their roots to these companies.

All of them are part of Williamsport's continuing growth into a diversified, small metropolitan area in a rural setting. Agriculture has never dominated the region because of the limited amount of tillable land. The bituminous and anthracite coal deposits both just miss the area, and any gas or oil that might be present has been largely unmolested because of geologic and economic factors. The one natural resource that put Williamsport on the map—lumber—was overexploited, as was common practice.

Since starting as an "outpost" on the Susquehanna River, the Williamsport area has grown to nurture 219 manufacturing firms with more than 14,500 employees in 1995. There are over 2,500 businesses. Lycoming County has over $340 thousand in average annual payroll.

The organizations whose stories are detailed on the following pages have chosen to support this important literary and civic project. They illustrate the variety of ways in which individuals and their businesses have contributed to the growth and development of Williamsport and Lycoming County. The civic involvement of the area's businesses, learning institutions, and local government, in partnership with its citizens, has made it a first-class place to live and work.

SUSQUEHANNA HEALTH SYSTEM

In July, 1994, an alliance was formed among three area hospitals, signaling the beginning of a new era in healthcare for the region. This alliance, called Susquehanna Health System, brought together The Williamsport Hospital & Medical Center, Divine Providence Hospital and Muncy Valley Hospital, along with all their subsidiaries, into one fully integrated healthcare system. This System provides high quality, compassionate, accessible and cost effective healthcare to thousands of residents in the region, and has received national recognition for its healthcare leadership. In addition to the three hospitals, the System includes Susquehanna Home Care, Susquehanna Physician Services, The Williamsport Area Ambulance Service and Muncy Valley Skilled Nursing Unit.

Although Susquehanna Health System is relatively young, the hospitals that make up the System are very much a part of the area's rich history, and have a long standing tradition of providing care to many generations of area families.

Sister Jean Mohl, chairperson, Board of Directors, and Donald R. Creamer, president and chief executive officer, are considered the architects of Susquehanna Health System.

A Growing Area Has Need Of A Place To Care For Its Sick And Injured

In the early 1800's, Williamsport was a tiny borough along the Susquehanna River surrounded by vast tracts of rich pine, hemlock and hardwoods that were in great demand to help feed the young nation's need for lumber. As sawmills began to spring up along the river, more and more workers came to the area looking to make a living in the new lumber industry. By the 1870's, Williamsport had become the lumber capital of the world. The population had grown dramatically, and with this growth came an increased incidence of sickness and injury. The sick were cared for in their homes by family members, and workers, who were injured on the job, were often treated in the boardinghouse rooms where they lived. Following several industrial accidents that occurred in the early 1870's, members of the Lycoming County Medical Society decided that it was time for a hospital where patients could be fed and cared for in a clean environment.

The Williamsport Hospital Incorporated

In 1873, upon petition by members of the Lycoming County Medical Society and 23 leading citizens of the community, the Lycoming County Court granted a Charter establishing The Williamsport Hospital. Despite the initial enthusiasm among community leaders for the facility, interest quickly cooled when these people were asked for money to purchase a building and beds. Eventually, James H. Perkins, a lumberman and former mayor, contributed half of the initial cost, and a three-story brick building on Elmira Street between Fourth and Edwin Streets was purchased. The first hospital in Williamsport opened its doors around April 1, 1878.

This hospital was, in reality, not much more than a clean boardinghouse intended for charity patients who had no suitable residence in Williamsport. A husband and wife fed and bathed patients in return for free living quarters. Physicians preferred to treat patients in their homes since they knew there was greater likelihood of being paid by those patients. During the first year of operation, the 20 or so physicians in the community admitted only nine patients to the hospital, and only four in the second year.

The hospitals of Susquehanna Health System, clockwise from top, The Williamsport Hospital, Divine Providence Hospital and Muncy Valley Hospital.

Dr. Rita B. Church came to Williamsport as the first administrator of The Williamsport Hospital.

Medical professionals recognized that in order to be successful, the hospital needed to be guided by someone with medical training. Dr. Jean Saylor, who had been active with the hospital, convinced Dr. Rita B. Church, a former college classmate, to come to Williamsport and run the fledgling hospital. With Dr. Church on the premises, hospital use increased dramatically, and this in turn created a shortage of nurses. The two doctors organized a training course for student nurses, establishing one of the first nursing schools in the state. The first student, Alta J. King, graduated in 1884, and for nearly 100 years, The Williamsport Hospital School of Nursing continued to provide the region with highly skilled nurses.

That same year, the hospital began looking for a larger building. A house on Pine Street near Fifth Avenue was purchased. Although this facility was larger, it had drawbacks. A nearby railroad created a lot of noise that was distracting to ill patients, and when the flood of 1889 filled the building with three feet of muddy water, the board of managers decided that it was time to find a more appropriate location. Eventually, a large tract of land, called Old Oaks Park, in the vicinity of Louisa and Campbell Streets and Rural Avenue was being opened for development. The board of managers purchased an entire city block and built a new facility that was opened in 1891. Over 100 years later, the main building of the hospital is still located on this site and is today The Williamsport Hospital campus of Susquehanna Health System.

Muncy Valley Hospital Founded

As the city of Williamsport was growing, so too were the surrounding areas. From this growth came the need for a medical facility to serve the increasing population in the eastern end of Lycoming County. Bad roads and long distances made traveling to The Williamsport Hospital almost impossible. Recognizing the need for the community to have its own hospital facility, twelve physicians from the Muncy, Hughesville and Montgomery areas worked together to establish a hospital in Muncy.

This small 20-bed facility opened in 1923 in a Victorian residence, that was originally the Noble family mansion on East Water Street. Dr. T. Kenneth Wood, a prime mover for the founding of the hospital, served as president. The facility cost $10,000, and with its opening, local residents felt they had created the ultimate in medical care.

Over the next two decades, the hospital was directed by a board composed exclusively by physicians. To help bring a new dimension of thought about healthcare to the facility, lay members of the community were admitted to the hospital board in 1940. In fact, it is believed that the leadership of two of these men, Earl D. Buck and W. Charles Walters, guided the campaign organization, administrative leadership, manpower and construction plans that were needed to meet the increasing demands being placed on the young hospital. In 1945, the hospital board agreed to undertake a new building program. Spurred by generous community support, the hospital began the construction of what is today the Muncy Valley Hospital campus of Susquehanna Health System.

Religious Order Establishes Divine Providence Hospital

Around the end of WW II, a suburban exodus was beginning in the city of

A group of physicians who co-founded Muncy Valley Hospital are pictured in front of the Hospital's first home located in the Noble family mansion.

Williamsport. As the population began moving to the outlying areas, particularly the eastern end of the city, the seeds of a new hospital were being sown by a religious order. Sister Mary Theresilla Hills, a native of Williamsport and a Sister in the Order of the Sisters of Christian Charity, who was in the city on a teaching assignment, reported to her motherhouse the need to "provide a place where the sick and injured could be treated in accordance with the mercy and compassion of Christ, coupled with the best principles of medical practice."

Two campaigns were conducted to build this Catholic hospital, one in 1945 - 46 and the other in 1948 - 49. They generated tremendous support from the community and business members and met both goals. On June 27, 1948, ground was broken at 1100 Grampian Boulevard on the border of the city of Williamsport and Loyalsock Township. The new 185-bed facility was dedicated on May 20, 1951. It opened its doors on June 1, 1951 under the direction of Sister Emilene Wehner, S.C.C., and is today the Divine Providence Hospital campus of Susquehanna Health System.

The Years Of Growth

Over the ensuing years, the three hospitals continued to thrive, adding new services and advanced technology to ensure area residents had the best possible medical care.

At The Williamsport Hospital, the rehabilitation and physical medicine center was established in 1961. The tremendous success of the center led to the current five story Gibson Rehabilitation Center which opened in 1970. During the 1960's this hospital created a mental health unit and initiated the first intensive care unit in central Pennsylvania. In medicine, advances were being made in treatment of heart patients, and in the early 1970's the hospital established a cardiopulmonary department that became the foundation for the System's cardiac surgery program of today. As more and more physicians began to specialize in various areas of medicine, a shortage of family practice physicians developed. To train a new generation of skilled family practice physicians, The Williamsport Hospital, in 1972, established the Family Practice Residency Program and became the first hospital in the northern half of the state to organize such a program. The Family Practice Residency Program continues to provide skilled family practitioners, many of whom locate in the region and provide medical support to rural communities.

Sisters of Christian Charity, including Sister Mary Therisilla (at right) take part in ground breaking ceremonies for an early expansion project at Divine Providence Hospital.

At Muncy Valley Hospital, the professional staff of the hospital increased to 14 physicians by 1951, and there was a consulting staff of various specialties including surgery, internal medicine, genito-urinary, eye, plastic surgery, x - ray, obstetrics, pediatrics, orthopedics, ear, nose, throat, and dental needs. In 1953, the Noble mansion that housed the original hospital was renovated and opened as a geriatric unit. An east wing was added to the hospital in 1957 and in 1968, the second floor of the east wing was completed. A new geriatric ward was established with money from a $45,000 grant from the County Commissioners, the beginning of what is today a comprehensive and modern Skilled Nursing Unit. Through Susquehanna Health System this facility has been expanded and renovated, and continues to provide area residents skilled nursing care in their own community.

At Divine Providence Hospital, construction began in 1958 on the first expansion of facilities; this project included a medical library, chapel, convent, auditorium and administrative offices. The laboratory, radiology and dietary departments expanded and bed capacity increased. A psychiatric inpatient unit opened in the early 1960's, the first step toward the future comprehensive mental health program that Divine Providence Hospital would establish. The 1960's also saw the opening of an intensive care unit, and the renovation of the obstetric unit. To keep up with expanding community needs, the hospital also began construction of a Health Services Building to house physicians offices, an outpatient pharmacy and community health services. Several regional services also began in the 1970's, including the Francis V. Costello Dialysis Center and the Cancer Treatment Center, and a Digestive Disease Center in 1976. In 1981, Divine Providence Hospital along with several other hospitals, formed a nonprofit corporation to provide mobile computerized tomography scanning services to 10 hospitals in northcentral Pennsylvania. This was the first such service in this area and, for its time, the largest nonprofit scanning corporation in the nation.

Demonstratng SHS's emphasis on providing high quality, compassionate care, a nurse visits with a patient while taking a blood pressure reading.

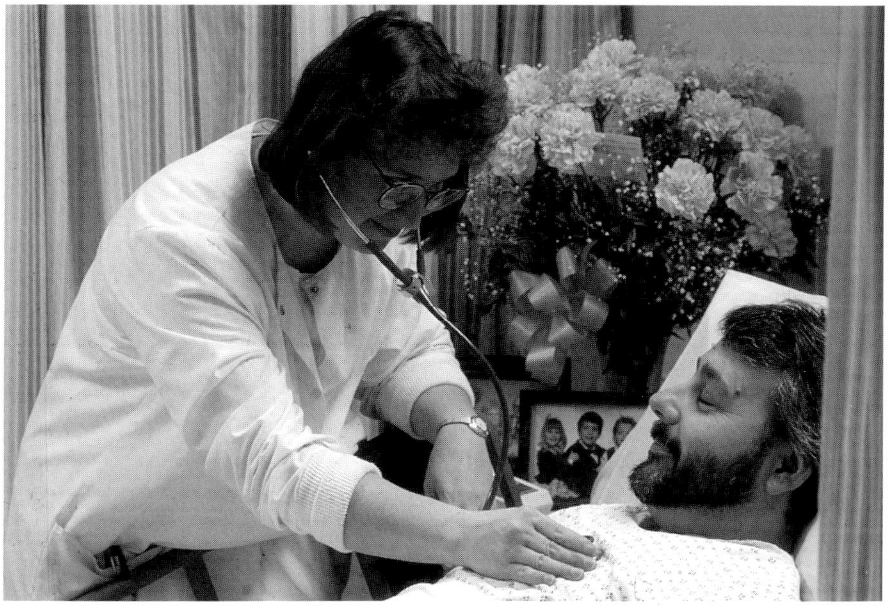

A Spirit Of Cooperation

For years these hospitals enjoyed a spirit of cooperation, often lending each other equipment and sharing technology. A note in The Williamsport Hospital's employee newsletter dated March 1951 congratulated the Muncy Valley Hospital on the opening of its new addition, and expressed the hope that "the hospitals of Lycoming County will enjoy full cooperation with one another in their joint effort to provide good hospital care... a unity of purpose among hospitals is essential to the voluntary hospital system."

A Partnership For Healthy Communities

The 1990's brought a period of major change to healthcare and many smaller hospitals began looking to associate with larger hospitals to strengthen their chances of survival. In 1991, Muncy Valley Hospital entered into a partnership with Divine Providence Hospital. Then, over the next few years Sister Jean Mohl, president of Divine Providence Hospital, and Donald R. Creamer, president of The Williamsport Hospital & Medical Center, along with board members from the hospitals, began a series of discussions that would eventually lead to the creation of Susquehanna Health System (SHS). The architects of this alliance, Sister Jean Mohl, the first chairperson of the Board of Directors of SHS, and Donald R. Creamer, the first president and chief executive officer, were committed to creating a seamless, highly integrated health system that would eliminate costly duplication of services and enhance the quality of care through the consolidation of these services. In 1996, the health system received national recognition from the VHA (formerly Voluntary Hospitals of America) for its healthcare leadership in the creation of a model healthcare delivery network serving the region. SHS is directed by an 18 member board comprised of an equal number of representatives, selected by the corporate parents, of each participating hospital system. These volunteer board members live and work in the region they serve.

For the community, the most visible aspect of SHS has been the consolidation of services. While some SHS services are available at all three hospital campuses, specialized services have been concentrated on the hospital campus that has already established itself as a Center of Excellence for that particular service. On The Williamsport Hospital campus, Centers of Excellence include Susquehanna Heart Center, WorkCenter, Sports Medicine, The Birthplace and Gibson Rehabilitation Center. Centers of Excellence on the Divine Providence Hospital campus include Susquehanna Cancer Center, the Behavioral Health Center and Dialysis Center, and on the Muncy Valley Hospital campus, a Skilled Nursing Unit. The System also operates the LifeCenter™, a community health promotion and education facility, located at Lycoming Mall and Susquehanna Health Source at the James V. Brown Library.

As SHS moves into the next century, the System continues to adapt to the changing needs of healthcare, caring for the sick and injured, but is also channeling increased efforts into community health improvement through wellness programs, disease prevention and early detection. Over 200 physicians in 40 specialties, along with numerous healthcare workers, educators, staff and volunteers, working in cooperation with community agencies and social service organizations, are out in the cities and suburbs, the schools and churches, senior centers, libraries and even the shopping mall, providing programs and services in our effort to fulfill Susquehanna Health System's mission to make the community we serve the healthiest community in the United States.

TEXTRON LYCOMING

The financial crisis of 1907 spawned a Williamsport company that not only participated in the birth of the automobile age but also became a pioneer in the air age.

That year Demorest Manufacturing Company (a general engineering business founded in 1845, which had grown to manufacture bicycles, typewriters, sewing machines, duplicators, gas irons, and platen printing presses) went bankrupt. It was then reorganized as Lycoming Foundry and Machine Company, with A.H. Ahles as president. John A. McCormick, who became a vital ongoing figure in the enterprise's development, was secretary/treasurer.

On the advice of prominent industrialist Hugh Chalmers, McCormick spent the early months of 1909 negotiating contracts to make engines for firms that assembled automobiles. The first order came from Velie Motor Corporation of Illinois to manufacture four-cylinder units from Velie's design.

Within a year Lycoming Foundry and Machine Company was producing engines for Velie, Hatfield, Apple, and others. Garrett Cochran became president in 1915, and the versatile McCormick took on the added duties of general manager. At the same time, a large expansion of the work force was initiated to produce the first Lycoming-designed motor for Dort automobiles.

The popularity of Lycoming engines continued to grow. In 1917 alone, 15,000 engines were built for Army trucks, ambulances, and other vehicles. They additionally powered the Martin-Perry delivery wagons, and Koehler one-ton and one-and-a-half-ton trucks.

Two years later 1,000 units were shipped to England—as well as U.S. sales to International Harvester, Federal, White, Republic, Stewart, Norwalk, Relay, Corbett, and Massey-Harris. Orders for 60,000 engines in 1919-1920 increased the work force to 2,000.

Small manufacturers of cars that joined the ranks of Lycoming-motor users included Dagmar and Roamer. Bradley-Ford used them in its hearses. Major customers in the southern United States were Piedmont Company in Virginia and Tulsa Company in Oklahoma for car engines; Southern Company in North Carolina for truck engines; and Texas Motors for both. Growth permitted boldness, and when Willys-Overland needed a large number of engine-block castings, Lycoming Foundry took the order and erected a large new facility to meet the added demand.

The reorganized and refinanced organization became Lycoming Manufacturing Company in May 1920, with McCormick remaining as general manager. Frank A. Bender, who was to play an important role in Lycoming's expansion, was named chief engineer. Having joined the operation in 1911 as a blueprint boy, Bender subsequently designed a new four-cylinder engine. The unit, which went into production in 1922, was used in the Gardner, Bush, Auburn, and Elcar automobiles.

Yellow, Checker, and Henry cabs all used Lycoming power plants in 1924. The following year Bender was promoted to assistant general manager, and E.D. Herrick was promoted to chief engineer. An innovative Lycoming straight-eight-cylinder motor was first used in the 1925 Auburn; Elcar and Apperson used the same engine in 1926. A cooperative Bender/Herrick effort produced the firm's six-cylinder unit that became the standard engine in other models of the Auburn, Elcar, and Gardner. Other illustrious automobiles that were powered by Lycoming engines were Locomobile, Cord, Duesenberg, Kissell, Paige, Graham, and McFarlan.

In the early 1920s the corporation also had begun serving the American commercial and residential market when it joined forces with the long-respected Williamsport Radiator Company, maker of the famous "Spencer Boilers." By the middle of the decade Lycoming Manufacturing Company employed

The Lycoming eight-cylinder engine assembly line. Engines were used in automobiles such as the Gardner, Elcar, and Auburn.

This 1936 Cord was powered by a Lycoming V-8 engine, which developed 115 horsepower at 3,500 r.p.m.

Stinson 0-49. *Designated the L-1 by the U.S. Army, this aircraft was powered by the Lycoming R-680 radial engine.*

Piper • Malibu Mirage. Designed for high altitude flight, this modern, pressurized general aviation aircraft is powered by a Lycoming T10-540-AE2A engine.

2,500 persons with a $10,000 daily payroll to produce 57 different types of motors.

Errett L. Cord, president of Auburn Motors, in building a transportation empire acquired Lycoming Manufacturing Company in 1927. He assumed the chairmanship from J.B. Graham and named McCormick president. As that also was the year Charles A. Lindbergh made the first solo flight across the Atlantic, it was no coincidence that Cord decided that Auburn's new subsidiary should enter the aircraft-engine industry.

Designs were started in 1928 on new marine, aircraft, and industrial motors. Lycoming-powered boats had won many trophies and gold cups in important races in the 1920s, and continued to do so in the 1930s. As a marine-engine showpiece, Lycoming souped up an Auburn-6 to 180 horsepower, and created such a hit in 1936 that it was mass-produced. Customers for engines with 45 to 330 horsepower included Penn-Yan, Elco, Wheeler, and Horace Dodge.

The corporation also served the industrial and agricultural fields, developing improved liquid-cooled stationary engines whose farm applications included use in a John Deere combine. Throughout industry a four-cylinder, 30-horsepower Lycoming unit was used primarily as a standby power plant for the generation of electricity.

Design work on the first Lycoming aircraft engine resulted in a conventional nine-cylinder radial engine with 680-cubic-inch displacement. The R-680 was an immediate success, and the first Lycoming-powered airplane flew at Williamsport in 1929. The engine soon powered the Beech-designed TravelAir and the Stinson Tri-motor used by Ludington Airline, National Airlines, and the Boston and Maine Airways—the earliest scheduled airlines in the United States. In addition to airline and personal aircraft of the period, the R-680 also powered several military trainers—including the well-known Stearman. During its period of manufacture, 25,000 of the engines were built.

In company boardrooms and private offices around the country, the many facets of the evolving air industry were prime topics of discussion; consequent decisions resulted in actions that would have immediate and long-range effects on Lycoming Manufacturing and Williamsport. The organization's future was effected in 1933, when Errett L. Cord gained control of Aviation Corporation and made it a subsidiary of Cord Corporation. Two years later he sold his controlling interest in Cord Corporation to Victor Emanuel, who immediately began to restructure the Cord subsidiaries. By 1939 Aviation Corporation owned all former assets—including Aviation Manufacturing Corporation and its subsidiary, Lycoming Manufacturing Company. In 1941 Aviation Manufacturing Corporation was dissolved, and Lycoming Manufacturing Company became a direct division of Aviation Corporation. The latter was renamed Avco Manufacturing Corporation in 1947, then Avco Corporation in 1959.

Meanwhile, in Williamsport, other important changes were taking place. Smith Engineering, a Lycoming Manufacturing Company subsidiary, in 1933 introduced the first mechanical, controllable propeller. (Over 84,000 eventually were produced.) The following year responsibility for automobile engines was largely removed from Williamsport to a Cord Corporation plant in Indiana. Also in 1934 W. Hubert Beal had become president of Lycoming Manufacturing Company—after having served as its sales manager since 1919, with the added duties of secretary since 1927. E.D. Herrick was promoted to general manager; three years later he was elected president.

In 1938, following up on its successful R-680 engine, the firm developed the flat, opposed-cylinder 0-145 aircraft engine. In the years that followed a complete series of four-, six-, and eight-cylinder engines, with up to 450 horsepower, was developed. They were used in aircraft produced by Piper, Beech, Ryan, and Taylorcraft, and became the standard for all leaders in the general-aviation aircraft industry. The company scored another coup in 1938 when Igor Sikorsky flew the first successful helicopter built in the United States. He used a four-cylinder, 75-horsepower Lycoming GO-145 engine.

The corporation's 12- and 24-cylinder, liquid-cooled engines were designed at 1,200 and 2,400 horsepower, respectively, prior to World War II. During that crisis the Williamsport facility became deeply involved in the research and development of larger units. Construction of a modern new laboratory began in 1943 to manufacture and test increasingly larger engines, including the X0-1230. By the end of the war Lycoming was experimenting with the world's largest piston engine with 36 cylinders at 5,000 horsepower—the famous XR-7755.

As the United States supported the Allies and then entered World War II, the firm played a vital role: Propellers for military aircraft were produced as well as thousands of engines in 30 versions. Its motors powered Vultee, Stinson, Curtiss-Wright, Cessna, and Beechcraft training, liaison, and observation planes. The Stearman trainer, with a Lycoming engine, was used to train more pilots than any other aircraft during the war. The durable, reliable R-680 became known as "the old sewing machine that goes and goes and goes."

And "the best air-cooled engine on the market," accordinq to Colonel Herrington, was the 0-435, 175-horsepower Lycoming Tank Unit used in the Marmon-Herrington tanks. Parts for the Packard-Merlin tank engines were also manufactured under subcontract.

In the ensuing years Avco Lycoming Williamsport continued to develop and build engines for general aviation, including some of the best-known single- and twin-engine utility aircraft in the business. Subcontract work for other manufacturers has been also a continuous part of the company's activities and was particularly helpful in the late 1940s and through the 1950s when aircraft-engine demand was low. As an example, Hall Scott engines for buses were manufactured during most of 1946 in a program with ACF-Brill Motors.

The company's defense work, however, never completely stopped. Parts for the Wright Aeronautical and the Pratt & Whitney radial aircraft engines, then being used by the airlines and the military, were built under subcontract from 1947 until the late 1950s. By that time gas-turbine engines claimed the large aircraft engine market, and Dr. Anselm Franz began designing a Lycoming gas-turbine unit.

Several new endeavors began in Williamsport in 1948. The 0-290, four-cylinder opposed aircraft engine was adapted to use in ground power units, enabling it to start aircraft such as the mammoth B-36 bomber. Production continued into the 1950s, and over 15,000 units were manufactured. Connecting rods for the Ford Motor Company were also produced.

About this time as well, Lycoming's boiler-building unit—Spencer—reentered the residential market. In 1949 the two units were combined to form the Lycoming-Spencer Division of Avco Manufacturing Corporation.

When the Korean War erupted in 1950, the government stepped up its orders for small aircraft and helicopters. Within a few months the demand for Lycoming engines led to the founding of a new plant in Stratford, Connecticut, and the division's turbine operation was relocated there in 1952. That same year Floyd Bird moved to Williamsport as general manager, serving in that position until 1966.

As a part of the country's rearmament program in the 1950s,

Textron Lycoming T10-540-AE2A certified aircraft engine. Dual turbochargers, dual intercoolers.

The Williamsport Lycoming Manufacturing Company plant in 1936.

Textron Lycoming's Williamsport facility. Photo 1994.

Lycoming Williamsport continued to build mobile auxiliary-power units and air-cooled Continental engines for medium tanks—which it had obtained the rights to produce at the beginning of the decade. The latter engine was manufactured under a government contract until 1955.

Under subcontract, in 1952 Lycoming initiated production of rotor components for the Piasecki H-21 helicopter. When the CH-46 Sea Knight helicopter was developed about 1960, the corporation obtained the subcontract to manufacture rotor components, which continued to be made in Williamsport into the 1980s.

Beginning in the late 1950s, geared supercharging was incorporated into Lycoming general-aviation engines to increase power output and provide for flight in the middle altitudes above 10,000 feet. Turbocharging, a more efficient method of compressing the thin air at high altitudes, was first used with Lycoming engines during the 1960s. The innovation utilized engine exhaust gases to turn the air compressor, and allow cruise flight at altitudes above 20,000 feet.

During the 1950s, 1960s, and 1970s Lycoming-powered aircraft continued in U.S. Army use. The Beech U-8 Seminole, a high-performance, all-weather courier that could easily be converted to an ambulance plane, and the Hughes Osage, a two-place helicopter used for pilot training,

In addition to its military business, Lycoming Williamsport provided opposed-cylinder, air-cooled engines for both helicopters and an increasing number of fixed-wing, general-aviation airplanes. By 1963, when the Avco Lycoming Division was separated into Avco Lycoming Williamsport and Avco Lycoming Stratford divisions, the reciprocating engines made in Williamsport were being used by most major manufacturers of small aircraft. During the 1960s and 1970s, as general-aviation demands increased over previous decades, these reciprocating engines were utilized to power aircraft in countries throughout the world.

The 1970's became the peak years for the general aviation industry. Thousands of general aviation aircraft were produced by major aircraft manufacturers such as Beech, Cessna, Mooney, Piper, and many others. Due to the large volume of airplanes produced during this period there was also an increased demand for Lycoming engines. New engine production reached a peak level of more than 17,000 engines a year. The requirement for Remanufactured engines and replacement service parts also increased as flight hours grew to an all time high.

With the advent of the 1980's new aircraft and engine production started into a long decline that still exist today due to a saturated market place and the financial impact of product liability laws. This, along with a general decline in the world economy negatively impacted Lycoming's core business of only manufacturing engines for new aircraft.

In 1987, Textron purchased the assets of AVCO Corporation which included Lycoming and the Williamsport facility.

Textron recognized there would no longer be a large enough demand for new Lycoming engines to support and maintain its manufacturing facility and skilled work force in Williamsport without making some strategic changes. With more than 250,000 Lycoming engines already in service, Lycoming determined there would be a significant market demand for factory overhauled engines. Lycoming developed and marketed its very successful "Lycoming Overhaul Engine Program" which now produces more than 2,500 overhaul engines a year.

Lycoming continues to offer a full line of four, six and eight cylinder engines ranging from 100 to 400 horsepower. Lycoming powers more than 80% of the new general aviation aircraft being produced throughout the world, including many countries that are developing general aviation aircraft like Brazil, China, India, Pakistan and Russia.

Lycoming's world-wide distribution network provides New Service, Remanufactured, and Overhaul Engines and service parts to all corners of the globe.

Today, due to changes in the product liability laws and the advancing age of the general aviation fleet, there is a growing demand for new piston powered aircraft. The excellent reputation of Lycoming engines places Williamsport based Lycoming in the enviable position of supplying most of this new demand.

KEYSTONE FILLER & MFG. CO.

Father and son Elisha and Richard Gray formed Keystone Paint Company in 1877, after migrating to Muncy from Sharon, Ohio, to grind black slate located along the river and make it into paint at a mill up the Muncy Canal.

In 1882 Levi Hill and John F. Leinbach bought into the enterprise, which was incorporated the following year. Elisha was the first president, Richard served as treasurer, and Levi was made secretary. Richard became president a short time later. In 1888 Hill and Leinbach left Keystone and purchased interests in one of several rival companies, none of which survived the turn of the century.

That same year Keystone constructed a 40- by 50-foot building with a 20- by 30-foot engine room. Six hundred tons of black filler and 10,000 gallons of black lead paint were produced annually. Within a few years the plant was 200 feet long, but two-thirds of it blew down in a strong wind in 1896.

The current facilities of Keystone Filler & Mfg. Co. after the 1982 expansion program, which added new factories and modern drying, screening, and grinding equipment.

The original building of Richard Gray's Keystone Paint Company was located at the junction of the Muncy and Pennsylvania canals. In 1888 the plant was moved to a new building constructed along the Reading Railroad adjacent to the depot to make it more convenient for shipping.

Following Richard Gray's death in 1900, the plant was acquired by A. DeLong and later by John L. Barbour. In 1934 it was sold to Cordeen C. Pfleegor, who incorporated it under Pennsylvania law as Keystone Filler & Mfg. Co. Although paint manufacturing had been discontinued, shale was being ground (until 1960), and paint fillers were still made. An anthracite-burning coal stoker was manufactured for a short period in Muncy.

In the late 1930s and early 1940s the owner's sons joined him in the business.

About 1938 Pfleegor developed a semianthracite coal filler, a lightweight product used in hard-rubber battery cases. During that time period as well, a grinding complex was put into a plant near Watsontown to produce finely ground filler for the record industry—which used red shale from that area. In the early 1950s the entire factory was purchased and made part of Keystone.

A fine-grinding plant was installed in 1951 in Muncy to produce materials on a custom basis. The machinery uses high-temperature, high-pressure steam, or compressed air to produce superfine materials.

Cordeen C. Pfleegor, Sr. died in 1957. His sons, Cordeen C. Jr. and Charles D., assumed management of the company. Both Cordeen C. Jr. and Charles are now deceased. Charles' son, David W. Pfleegor is now president of the company.

Property and equipment expansion continued during the 1960s, due to increasing battery box-filler demands in the United States and Mexico. Although plastic battery cases introduced in the 1970s caused a decline in use of ground anthracite coal, it continues as a principal company product.

In the early 1970s Keystone began supplying metallurgical carbon products to the steel industry. This manufacture ranges from high-purity, selectively mixed anthracite coals to high-carbon metallurgical cokes, all available in different configurations.

Major expansion programs were undertaken in 1982 and 1995. New factories were erected and modern drying, screening, and grinding equipment was acquired to be used by 50 employees.

ANCHOR/DARLING VALVE COMPANY

On August 29, 1859, the oil industry was born when Colonel Drake drilled the first successful well near Titusville, Pennsylvania. Though technological change was much slower then than we are accustomed to today, in just three decades the embryonic industry had grown to the point where new companies were being created primarily to serve its burgeoning needs. In 1888 one of them was the Darling Pump and Manufacturing Company, Inc., started in Williamsport because it was centrally located to the young oil fields.

Jonathan Louis Hough II, a clerk for the Pennsylvania Railroad, which had begun limited transportation of oil, and Ralph H. Thorne, a telegraph operator, started the company. Several members of the Darling family, who were Thorne's relatives, made a small investment in the enterprise based on their experience in oil.

The initial principal products were deep oil well pumps and supplies.

Within six years the first small plant was inadequate and a new site was purchased a short distance away along a Pennsylvania Railroad branch.

By the early 1900s the business had grown considerably and the two original partners split the responsibility; Hough was in charge of sales and accounting while Thorne directed manufacturing. C.W. Huling was secretary/accountant and A.G. Smith was sales manager. Harry Darling was plant superintendent.

The first fire hydrants were made in 1902 and were a gate type with a metal-to-metal shutoff. A hydrant with a frost jacket followed and then a compression type was designed by the company's Philadelphia sales agent.

As the valve and hydrant business increased, the firm gradually left the oil well supply business, except for the Darcova Valve and Pump Cups which were developed as an improvement over the leather cups in use early in the 20th century.

The original partners continued as active top management for nearly 30 years until J. Lewis Hough died in 1917. In 1918 the concern changed from a limited partnership to a corporation named Darling Valve and Manufacturing Company to more clearly identify the business. Robert Thorne became president, Marshall Hough, treasurer, and Huling, secretary.

In 1956 Darling entered the nuclear power field. Since then it has supplied a variety of valves ranging from the relatively straightforward needs of commercial demineralized cooling water services to the extremely sophisticated requirements of naval nuclear power components for primary loop service.

Growth and expansion required more capital, so on May 1, 1967, the estates of the founding families sold all their stock to the Philadelphia-based A.C. Forr Corporation. The firm had been founded in 1965 by Armin C. Frank, Jr., who became Darling president, and Robert A. Orr.

In 1969 the A.C. Forr Corporation acquired the Anchor Valve Company, located in San Francisco, and in 1973 the valve companies combined the names to Anchor/Darling Valve Company with divisions in Hayward, California, and Williamsport, Pennsylvania.

Today Anchor/Darling Valve Company has grown to become one of the world's foremost suppliers of high-specification, custom-engineered valves for critical applications. It is headquartered in Wynnewood, Pennsylvania, and has its manufacturing facilities in Williamsport.

Anchor/Darling Valve Company in 1982.

This carbon steel, air-motor-operated gate valve, as seen in Anchor/Darling's final assembly area, is one of many custom-engineered valves for use in such areas as radioactive, cryogenic, high-temperature, and high-pressure service throughout the world.

ALCAN CABLE

Alcan Cable had its beginning on May 1, 1939, when Central Cable Corporation began production in the former Susquehanna Silk Mill on Washington Avenue in Jersey Shore, Pennsylvania. The three Detwiler founders, David Roy, president; John G., treasurer; and William F. Jr., decided to specialize in manufacturing copper cables for utilities.

Jersey Shore was selected by the trio because of its ready access to a rapidly expanding market for the product. Pennsylvania had no other manufacturer of insulated wire and cable at the time.

The operation began with 50 to 60 young women operating braiding machines, which applied cotton to the wire. Then an asphalt coating, followed by one of wax, was applied.

An important factor in the growth of the company was the increasing impact of the Rural Electrification Administration, which spread electrical transmission lines into the countryside — using miles of cable. After John G. Detwiler became president in 1946, a major expansion step was taken with the opening of other plants.

New materials and processes were constantly evolving. When aluminum became a rival to copper in 1950, bare and weatherproof aluminum cable were added to the line.

Plastic cable covering emerged in late 1952, and a few months later the first neoprene continuous vulcanizing line was installed.

Central Cable Corporation became a wholly owned subsidiary of Alcan Aluminium Limited of Montreal, Canada, in 1963.

A fabrication plant was constructed in 1964 on a 25-acre site in Williamsport's Industrial Park to house a large new wire mill. Growth was rapid, and from 1966 to 1967 a total of seven bays were added to the building to provide more manufacturing and warehouse space on the east end of the facility.

In 1964 Alcan Cable Company constructed a 250- by 400-foot fabrication plant on a 25-acre site in Williamsport's Industrial Park. As shown here, after several additions the facility now houses over 350,000 square feet of manufacturing space.

The company's name was changed to Alcan Cable on January 1, 1966. Later that year construction of a modern wire-fabricating plant was started at Sunset/Whitney, California.

Also during 1966 plans were begun to build a high-speed rolling mill in a new addition to the Williamsport plant. The unique 100,000-ton-capacity Swedish rolling mill began producing a high-quality wire rod, the initial ingredient for manufacturing aluminum cable, in 1968; it is still one of the fastest methods used in the United States.

Alcan Cable's Jersey Shore plant.

In 1968 a new research and development building became operational, in order to develop better and more sophisticated cable coverings. Another structure was built in 1971 for use as the division office, until the division headquarters office later moved to Atlanta.

By 1995 the Alcan Cable facility in Williamsport had over 350,000 square feet of manufacturing space — including the 100,000-ton rod mill, a 40,000-ton cable plant, one research and development building. Its 300 employees operate the plant 24 hours a day, seven days a week, producing cable and aluminum rods known and used internationally.

EUREKA PAPER BOX COMPANY, INC.

Still located on Eureka Place, Eureka Paper Box Company, Inc., now occupies this expanded facility.

Eureka Paper Box Company, Inc., was founded in 1915 by Christian Stanton Knaur, John Lupert, and John Candor. The firm—located on Bridge Street, in the southern end of the Lowery Building—employed seven people making folding cartons: cake, candy, and food boxes; and other product containers. About three years later Knaur acquired Lupert's and Candor's interests in the enterprise. From the beginning annual sales ranged between $40,000 and $50,000, and the growing firm soon needed more space.

In 1925 it was moved to a 5,100-square-foot plant at 401 Eureka Place near Penn and Canal streets where 12 people were employed. A 13,000-square-foot section was added in 1933, at which time there were 23 employees. Sales escalated to $450,000 annually by 1950, and in 1952 a 5,600-square-foot office section was constructed.

Until 1962 printing was done on letterpress with cylinder and platen cutters. Brightwood folders folded the cut pieces. The plant then changed to offset printing. Between 1952 and 1968 Eureka had a steady uphill growth that saw annual sales reach $969,000.

A warehouse addition was built in 1968; however, a year later the 28,000 square feet were converted to production space for high-speed offset presses. More economical rolls of paper, instead of pre-cut sheets, began to be purchased in 1972. A new high-speed cutter produced 2,400 sheets per hour. Since 1968 annual sales have accelerated to three million dollars, and employees have stabilized between 50 to 62, including 10 office personnel.

In order to expand the market area, two companies were purchased by Eureka. On July 14, 1976, Tri-State Paper Box in Middletown, New York, was acquired. On December 6, 1979, Schiefer Packaging, Inc., in Syracuse, New York, was bought. While both plants make the same type of products as Williamsport, Middletown produces corrugated boxes, as well.

Although the customer base for each plant is a 300-mile radius, there are other customers throughout the United States, such as Stroehmann, Sylvania, San Giorgio, Johnson & Johnson, Purex, and Tastycake.

Founder Christian Stanton Knaur was active in his company until his death in 1946. His son, Christian Mowry Knaur, was vice-president from 1935 to 1946, then served as president for two years. He was then succeeded by his son, Raymond Mowry Knaur, who was president from 1948 to 1961. Perry Knaur, Raymond's brother, then served as president while Raymond was chairman of the board from 1961 to 1969. Raymond and Perry retired in 1969. Maude O. Knaur, Raymond's aunt—who had served as secretary/treasurer since 1946—also retired in 1969. Richard Wagner joined the firm at that point as secretary/treasurer. Richard M. Knaur, Raymond's son, became president and chairman of the board. In 1970 Charles Simek joined the firm as an officer.

Eureka Paper Box has grown as an extended family business, and many employees have been with the company for over 40 years.

The year was 1935 and the company's 23 employees pose in front of the 401 Eureka Place location.

GEORGE E. LOGUE, INC.

Starting with a backhoe he built in his basement, George E. Logue's enterprises evolved into a construction company that reached 200 employees and $10.5 million in annual sales.

The Williamsport native attended local schools, and received an engineering degree from Penn State University in 1951. His first employment was with International Harvester in Chicago, where he worked three years at the proving grounds. Desiring to return to Williamsport, Logue obtained a position with Sprout, Waldron & Company, remaining there for three years until he started his own business in 1957.

The entrepreneur's interest in Caterpillar took serious form with his purchase of a new Cat 933 in July of 1957, when he was in business as an excavating contractor. From its humble beginning - digging ditches - the construction company grew into a multifaceted enterprise completing multi-million dollar projects.

In 1968 a 68 acre tract of land along route 220 at the West End of Williamsport was acquired and an asphalt plant was erected. In 1972 the asphalt plant and assets of the M. L. Smith company in Loyalsock Township were purchased. With the only such facilities in the city, Logue built a substantial paving business - in addition to bridge and sewer construction in Central Pennsylvania.

Examples of the wide variety of projects include the extension and rebuilding of the Williamsport Lycoming County airport runway, reconstruction and widening of the Pleasant Gap-Centre Hall road, laying of the West End and Erie Ave. storm sewers in Williamsport and the Broad Ave. relief sewer in Altoona, construction of an eight mile sewer in Carlisle, ten miles of sewer in Hughesville, two waterline crossings of the Susquehanna River, construction of various bridges and dams in the area including the Dunwoody bridge which received a state award from Penn-Dot and the construction of the Grays Run Dam. Also included is the site development of various housing developments including Tules Run in Montoursville, the site development of the Walmart and Scott's Lo Cost in Montoursville, and the Sam's Club, Circuit City and Toys R Us at the Lycoming Mall along with all the utility work for a Sam's Club and Walmart in Altoona. Among demolition endeavors were the Old Main at Lycoming College, the County Court House, and the Campbell Street underpass. During any paving season, residents encountered Logue projects throughout the region.

George E. Logue

Today the Caterpillar collection numbers in excess of 50. The asphalt plants were sold to Koppers Company, Inc. (in

December 1983) and almost all of the construction equipment was sold at auction in March of 1984 to allow for expansion of the manufacturing activities. The construction company was rehabilitated by George Logue Jr. (Herman) shortly after the sale on a much smaller scale specializing in underground utilities and site development. The company now operates out of the old Carey McFall building at 120 South Arch Street in Montoursville along with utilization of various other properties in the area either owned or leased including the Wahoo Industrial Park, property on Fairfield Road and buildings and grounds leased from the Lycoming County Airport.

Logue designs & fabricates specialized parts and machinery for various clients throughout central Pa. Operating primarily as a job shop with some of the most advanced machining and fabricating capabilities, Logue employs approx. 25 skilled craftsmen at the manufacturing plant.

Logue's manufacturing business was inspired by the requests of his suppliers, customers and associates and his desire to build a better mousetrap. He has built various products ranging from sheet metal cutters to rocksplitters, with his largest product being a mechanical bombpicker for the U.S. Navy. Logue holds numerous patents on various truck body designs and construction equipment improvements. George Jr. also holds a patent on an erosion control product which is being marketed nationally. The construction company has grown back up to employing approx. 65 employees & growing, including Christopher Logue, P.E., a nephew of George Sr.

In 1994 Logue built a memorial to his brother and the other Veterans of Lycoming County lost in submarines during World War II. The memorial was erected at the entrance to the Wahoo Industrial Park developed by Logue and named after the submarine his brother Robert was lost on. In September of 1995 Logue went to Hokkaido Japan and erected a memorial at the site where the submarine was lost. Prior to this Logue had met the men that first spotted the Wahoo in the Sea of Japan and the pilots that bombed the submarine. He also spoke with fishermen that often get their nets tangled on the submarine. The Japanese government helped Logue locate the submarine and place a wreath at the site, along with helping with the construction of the memorial, both financially and emotionally.

On land in Gamble Township settled by his Grandfather Logue in 1884, the founder and his wife, Elizabeth, have raised ten children. There are several buildings which include a machine shop as well as a large structure that houses his collection of antique Caterpillar tractors.

George E. Logue, Jr.

PENNSYLVANIA COLLEGE OF TECHNOLOGY

Pennsylvania College of Technology offers students a rich tradition of excellence in technology-based education. Innovative education and programs that respond to real workplace needs have been offered here since the early part of this century. While its name has changed several times since those early days, the College has stayed true to one vision:

Shaping futures
through comprehensive learning opportunities
with distinction in technology education.

Machine Shop Instruction, March 1931

Williamsport Technical Institute

founded 1941

While 1941 was the year the Williamsport Technical Institute was formally established, programming actually had been in place since 1914, when a small high school industrial shop became home to adult education and training programs. Many of the first students to enroll were disabled veterans from World War I who needed immediate retraining.

In the 1920s, the focus shifted from industrial arts to vocational training. That shift helped combat the effects of the Depression in the 1930s. Cooperation between the school and local industry led to the development of a plan for attacking rising unemployment through retraining. "The Williamsport Plan" was copied throughout the United States and encompassed cooperative training of the Civilian Conservation Corps and the National Youth Administration.

World War II led to even more change in the 1940s. Training to meet defense industry needs was crucial; so the institute operated on a 24-hour-a-day schedule. Part of that training involved programs for individuals with handicaps, who were a big part of the war effort. Even before the "G.I. Bill" was passed in 1944, training also was being offered for returning World War II vets. The war production training and special training for disabled veterans returning from WWII led to the institute becoming one of the nation's largest providers of training and retraining for people with physical handicaps.

Williamsport Area Community College

founded 1965

The passage of the Community College Act of 1963 led to the establishment of Williamsport Area Community College, on the foundation of the former Williamsport Technical Institute. The College used the technical institute programs and facilities as the starting point for growth and development. Area school districts served as local sponsors for the Community College. By the 1970s service to those sponsoring districts included both credit and non-credit courses offered in Williamsport and at the new Earth Science Center near Allenwood, as well as at a variety of school district locations.

The 1980s brought more change. The Community College established a North Campus to serve needs of the residents of Pennsylvania's Northern Tier. Enrollment throughout the College was climbing steadily, with students coming from many areas outside the College's service area. While the physical plant grew and the enrollment expanded, local school districts became increasingly concerned about costs and the College faced eroding sponsor support. The City of Williamsport assumed the sponsor role on a temporary basis until 1989, when the College was named an affiliate of The Pennsylvania State University.

Pennsylvania College of Technology

founded 1989

As a Penn State affiliate, Penn College is realizing its full potential as Pennsylvania's premier technical college. Continuing in a tradition of excellence, Penn College is a strong force in higher education in Pennsylvania, offering certificate, associate and baccalaureate degree programs. Students from around the state, the nation, and the world are enjoying the benefits of state-of-the-art programs in traditional and emerging technologies.

Unique bachelor of science degree programs are providing new opportunities for students to build upon their technical background and advance into management and specialty positions. Regular, new additions to the Penn College program portfolio are training men and women, not only to meet existing workplace demands, but to prepare for the careers of tomorrow.

Present day Penn College, 1996

WWPA/WILLIAMSPORT RADIO CORPORATION

WWPA was conceived in 1946 when a group of local businessmen learned the FCC was going to allocate a Class-4 frequency to the area. Williamsport Broadcasting was formed with Harry J.W. Kiessling, president; William P. Wilson, treasurer; and stockholders George L. Stearns II, U.S. Congressman Alvin R. Bush, Carl F. Stroehmann, Ray L. Riley, Senator John C. Snowden, S. Dale Furst, and the Grit Publishing Company.

After three years of FCC hearings, WWPA was granted the 1340 frequency to operate a 250-watt AM station at 330 Government Place with the transmitter in South Williamsport. Area native Woodrow W. Ott, program director of WENY, Elmira, New York, joined the corporation as station manager.

Broadcasting began at 12:31 p.m. on Sunday, May 22, 1949. A CBS affiliate, Lycoming County's second station was middle of the road with a 6:30 a.m.-to-midnight schedule. Network favorites included "Arthur Godfrey," "Romance of Helen Trent," "Suspense," and "Lux Radio Theatre." Lowell Thomas brought world news to Williamsport. And Martin Jewelers made the first request for advertising time, 30 seconds before "The Jack Benny Show."

In addition to national programs and local news, WWPA strove to cover and support local programs and activities. "Sally Llson's Program," live from L.L. Stearns, was the first originating in Lycoming County about women's concerns. That year also brought the first of 35 continuous years of Penn State football broadcasts. Scholastic sports coverage was begun in football and basketball. The Eastern Baseball League Williamsport Grays and the Billies basketball games were covered live at home—and recreated by wire from the away games.

Summit Enterprises, Inc., acquired WWPA in March 1961. Ott became president, serving until his death in November 1975. His son, W. William Ott, was named president and general manager on January 19, 1976.

Sunday, February 13, 1977, saw four fires set in Williamsport. One totally destroyed Pine Street United Methodist Church. Another severely damaged the offices and studios of WWPA. For the remainder of the winter, the on-air staff operated from burned, damp studios; the office staff was housed at the Genetti Lycoming Hotel. An already-planned move to the old Growers' Market building at the foot of Market Street Bridge was accelerated, and the station moved into those quarters.

Its daytime power increased to 1,000 watts in 1965, and WWPA now serves all of Lycoming County. Since the mid-1970s it has become a highly promotional station that gives away automobiles, trips to Hawaii and Bermuda, plus lots of America's favorite prize—cash.

From the beginning, community involvement has been WWPA's forte. It is recognized as a leader in this area and supports over 100 local organizations. In 1980 it played an integral part in establishing the "Fanny in the Susquehanny" annual charity inner tube float down the river. The event has grown to include over 20,000 floaters and spectators, and this helps support several local charities.

Today WWPA is owned by Williamsport Radio Corporation along with sister station WVRT/FM 97.7 and is more aggressive than ever in developing community relations, strong ties with the Williamsport/Lycoming Chamber of Commerce and continues to be an integral part of the community with news talk and sports programming. WVRT/FM features new adult contemporary music and like WWPA is very innovative, ambitious and responsive to community needs.

Penn State Nittany Lions update has been broadcast by WWPA since 1949.

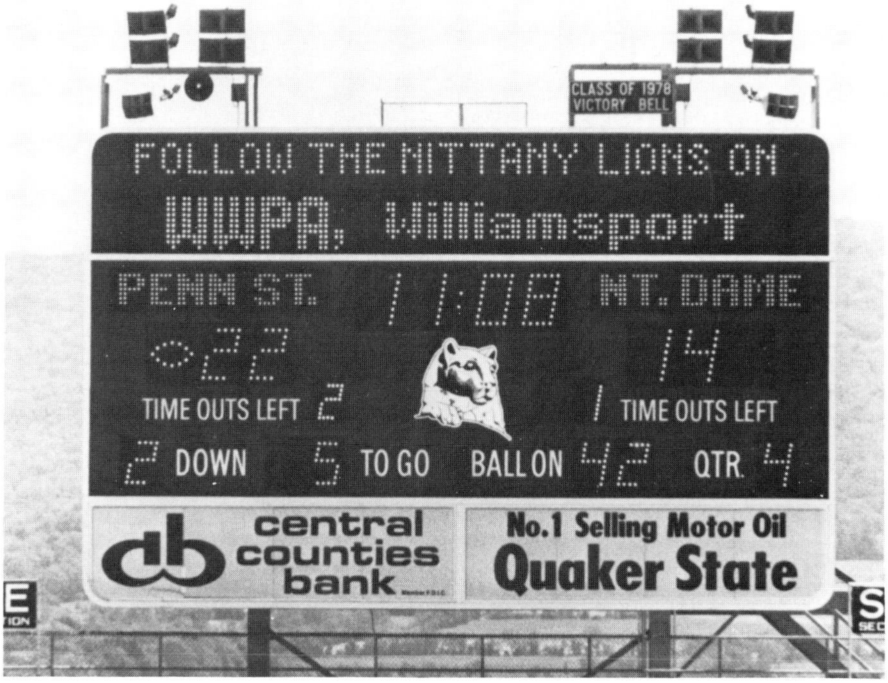

NORTHERN CENTRAL BANK

When Williamsport became a borough in 1806, there were no financial institutions to serve its banking needs. It was necessary to travel by horseback, stagecoach, or boat to Philadelphia or Baltimore to complete financial transactions. Often a messenger to one of these cities would buy supplies or pay bills for many Williamsport accounts.

By the 1830s the growing needs of the Williamsport community, as well as uncertain political and financial conditions at the national level, paved the way for a banking house in the area. In 1832 President Andrew Jackson eliminated the national banking system by vetoing the renewal of a charter for the Second United States Bank. He then gradually transferred government deposits to selected state-chartered institutions. This policy produced speculative situations in business and financial circles, resulting in the formation of many state-chartered banks.

The West Branch Bank was chartered in 1835 as the first banking house in Williamsport. The forerunner of Northern Central Bank, it occupied the old Eagle Hotel property in the city. John H. Cowden, a local businessman, was its first president. Shortly thereafter it moved to what is now part of L.L. Stearns and Sons.

As Williamsport continued to expand, the West Branch Bank also experienced rapid growth. Much of this growth could be attributed to the completion of the West Branch Canal, the advent of railroads, and the flourishing lumber industry.

With the enactment of the National Bank Act, the institution received a national charter in 1865 and became the West Branch National Bank. It was located at 309 Pine Street until 1917, at which time a handsome, white marble building on the northwest corner of Fourth and Pine streets was completed. Today it serves as Northern Central Bank's main office and NCB Financial Corporation's corporate headquarters.

While the West Branch National Bank was growing, other financial institutions were developing that would play an important role in Northern Central Bank's history. In April 1871 the Lycoming County Savings Bank, a private financial institution, was organized with J.P. Finley as president; four years later it was converted into a national bank with the title Lycoming National Bank.

Another private bank—Cochran, Payne and McCormick—was organized in April 1887 with J. Henry Cochran (lumberman, industrialist, and state senator) as president. E.R. Payne was the only Williamsporter ever to own a seat on the New York Stock Exchange. Henry Clay McCormick, a lawyer, once was Pennsylvania's attorney general. In 1897 the firm's name was changed to Cochran, McCormick and Cochran, and in 1909 the bank was transferred into the newly formed Northern Central Trust Company.

A most notable date in Northern Central Bank's history would have to be December 31, 1926, when the Lycoming Trust Company was formed. It began operations the next day as an amalgamation of the West Branch National Bank, then nearly a century old; the Lycoming National Bank; and the Northern Central Trust Company. James B. Graham was president of the combined banks. One other principal, Charles A. Schreyer, assistant secretary and trust officer, would later become president and chairman of Northern Central Bank and Trust Company.

The Susquehanna Trust and Safe Deposit Company was merged into the Lycoming Trust Company in 1930. Within a few years the branch offices previously maintained by West Branch National Bank,

West Branch National Bank, a forerunner of Northern Central Bank, under construction in 1916 at the corner of Fourth and Pine streets in Williamsport.

The same facility serves as the headquarters of NCB Financial Corporation as well as Northern Central Bank and its Center City consumer banking facility.

Susquehanna Trust and Safe Deposit Company, and Northern Central Trust Company (which had merged with Lycoming Trust Company in 1927) were all closed because of the financial strain on the newly formed bank.

The Bank Holiday in March 1933 gave financial institutions throughout the country many problems. In October the West Branch Trust Company was chartered to receive the liquid assets of Lycoming Trust Company, which had been placed on a restrictive operating basis by the Pennsylvania Department of Banking. In January 1934 the West Branch Bank & Trust Company was organized with assets of $4.5 million to succeed the West Branch Trust Company.

The next major event in Northern Central's history took place on November 4, 1963, when the West Branch Bank & Trust Company and the Bank of Newberry merged to form Northern Central Bank and Trust Company. Charles A. Schreyer was chairman of the board and president, with Woodrow A. Knight serving as board vice-chairman and senior vice-president. Knight assumed the position of president in 1967, with Schreyer maintaining the chairmanship until 1972.

With expansion taking place in Loyalsock Township, the institution established a branch at the corner of River Avenue and Washington Boulevard. Opened in June 1966, this third bank office proved to be a successful venture.

Northern Central Bank and Trust Company shortened its name to Northern Central Bank in 1975. John B. McMurtrie became president that year, and in 1978 succeeded Knight as board chairman.

During the 1970s Northern Central embarked on an ambitious expansion program through seven mergers and the opening of two new offices. In order of merger, they included Milton Bank and Safe Deposit Company, Athens National Bank, First Citizens National Bank of Montgomery, Susquehanna Valley Bank in Sunbury, First National Bank of Dushore, Guaranty Trust and Safe Deposit Company in Shamokin, and the First National Bank of Millville. The new offices included the Southgate Plaza office in Milton, and the Lycoming Mall office in Muncy Township. In the early 1980s this merger trend continued, involving Lewisburg National Bank, The Farmers National Bank of Rome, and The State Bank of Avis.

As the financial industry entered a period of revolutionary change in the early 1980s, marked by less restrictive regulatory policy, directors and officers of Northern Central Bank recommended that its shareholders approve the establishment of a holding company to take maximum advantage of broader opportunities for increased growth and profitability. In mid-1983 NCB Financial Corporation became a reality, with Northern Central Bank becoming a wholly owned subsidiary. This new entity could then consider an increasing number of nontraditional banking services under a more flexible capital structure and use more innovative and varied financial arrangements in mergers and acquisitions.

Shortly after its origination, NCB Financial Corporation became the parent organization of Tri-County National Bank of Middleburg. The holding company then consisted of two banks with 34 offices in nine counties, with total assets approximating $700 million.

Concurrent with the holding company formation, the bank significantly expanded its range of consumer services. The William Teller ATM network, which allows customers to do their banking 24 hours a day, became nationwide in scope by affiliating with the CashStream and CIRRUS ATM networks. The Discount Brokerage service offers investors the opportunity to buy and sell securities at a substantial cost reduction. The automobile-leasing program provides an alternative approach to traditional car purchasing. And a credit insurance subsidiary insures installment loan balances held by bank customers.

Further demonstrating its flexibility in responding to changes in the financial industry, NCB Financial Corporation formed Keystone Financial, Inc. This move strategically positioned the new holding company and its bank subsidiaries, now numbering five banks and several affiliate companies, to take full advantage of emerging trends in the financial industry, while meeting the ever-changing needs of its customers.

JAMES MEYER COMPANY

The James Meyer Company is a place where fine gold jewelry is designed and made by hand on the premises. Founded in 1970 by its namesake, the James Meyer Company has brought a level of innovation, craftsmanship, and service hitherto unknown in the region. In fact, so popular has the "James Meyer" style become, that numerous imitations have sprung up in the area in an attempt to follow the path of the originator.

But - to go back a little in time .... James was educated in the ancient languages and history at Haverford College, in sculpture and drawing at the Rhode Island School of Design, and at the Polytechneion in Athens on a Fullbright Scholarship. He taught briefly at Lycoming College, but left during the social revolution with a desire to be an expressive artist. The idea to make jewelry came from his friend Perry Adelson, the dentist, as a way to be an artist and make a living also.

So - in 1970, James opened a retail store and workshop in an obscure upstairs location on West Third Street. In 1978, the business moved to its present location at 441 Market Street, in an old commercial building previously used as an office by Dr. Allen Hannen. In the twenty-seven years since the business began, James' designs have found their way into many collections, most notably the Smithsonian in Washington, to many shows around the country, and to shows in Japan and Italy. His jewelry is noted for its fine design and craftsmanship, with references to nature and ancient art, and for its wearability and lasting beauty. His son Caleb Meyer, who worked in his shop for five years, has since opened his own jewelry design studio in Chestnut Hill, Pennsylvania.

James loves the area for its people, the beauty of the region, and the unhurried lifestyle it affords. He is proud to have been one of the "Founding Fathers" of the West Branch School, which opened in 1971 and continues to offer unique, open-classroom education in Williamsport.

George Washington belt buckle made in 1976 to commemorate the bicentennial. Collection of the Smithsonian Institute

Custom made rings in the traditional James Meyer style in 18k shown with sapphires, diamonds and rubies

James Meyer and Frank Shinko at the bench in 1971

Current staff of the JMC from left: Ann Snella, James Meyer, Stephanie Richards, Mary Herzenberg, Elise Craner, Chris Keenan

LYCOMING COLLEGE

Rev. Crever

Pres. Long

Lycoming College has a rich heritage, rooted in the liberal arts tradition and a commitment to service to others. Founded in 1812 as the Williamsport Academy, it is one of the 50 oldest colleges in the United States. Its original incorporation papers described its mission as "the Education of Youth in the English and other Languages, in the Useful Arts, Sciences and Literatures." It also accepted an obligation to offer an education, free of charge, to a number of poor children each year.

The Williamsport Academy began in a building located on the northwest corner of Academy Square, at West Third and West Streets. In the 1840's, its trustees moved it north to "The Hill" and built a new building that eventually would be the west wing of Old Main. Ironically, the move coincided with the growth of the public school movement and the relocated Academy fell on hard times. The Williamsport Town Council bought it in 1845 and soon put it up for sale. The school had always been non-sectarian but its founders and early administrators were often as not Presbyterian. In its time of crisis the Methodists stepped forward. The Reverend Benjamin H. Crever, a Methodist circuit rider serving the Williamsport area, decided his denomination should have the school. He worked hard to that end and in 1848 the Methodists, through their Baltimore Conference, purchased it. They renamed it Dickinson Seminary and it began to offer college preparatory courses. Crever never served the new Seminary as president, but his vision was so crucial to its transformation that he is considered its founder. Lycoming College continues to be related to the United Methodist Church.

Dickinson Seminary continued as a college preparatory school until 1929. In that year the President, the Reverend John R. Long, led the school to junior college status. Renamed the Williamsport Dickinson Junior College, it became the first fully accredited junior college in Pennsylvania in 1935. Long was not finished with his college. He believed it could become a four year baccalaureate institution, and in 1947 he led his school to that status. The new college continued the liberal arts tradition. It leaders chose the name "Lycoming" which is derived from an Indian word which means "Great Stream." Long served the college for 34 years, and put his vision of higher education on the institution. The Board of Trustees honored him for this vision by naming the College Library for him. The building stills bears his name but is now the administration building.

Lycoming College has evolved a great deal in the almost 50 years since its founding. It now offers bachelor of arts programs in 32 major fields, a Bachelor of Fine Arts in sculpture, Bachelor of Science degrees in biology and chemistry, and a Bachelor of Science in Nursing degree. It has sustained its excellent record of preparation of students for the professions of law and medicine, the Christian ministry and teaching. It has made great strides in technology and has wired its dormitories and classroom buildings so that every student and faculty and staff member can use its computer network, for internal uses and for access to the Internet. It has developed a new program in International Education and has exchange programs with a number of international educational institutions. And it has established an innovative internship program in the fields of business, accounting, and economics. In fact, fully two-thirds of its students have some kind of internship or practicum experience by the time they graduate.

It has also continued to expand its physical plant, with a new gymnasium in 1980 and a renovated center for the study of art in 1983. The most recent additions are the Heim Biology and Chemistry Building, opened in 1990, and a new quadrangle, established in 1995 between the Academic Center and the Heim Building.

These changes rest, however, on the stability and continuity of its mission. The words have changed somewhat since the Academy and Seminary, but the substance has not. Lycoming College remains committed to providing its students with a "distinguished baccalaureate education in the liberal arts," in a "coeducational, supportive, residential setting through programs that develop communication and critical thinking skills." Its students are "encouraged to develop and strengthen virtues and traits of character that enable, ennoble, and emancipate the human spirit while deepening commitment to those values that undergird civilization."

Heim Biology and Chemistry Building

LAMCO COMMUNICATIONS INC.

Communications has always been Lamco's business. For most of its corporate life, information was through the printed word. Today, however, the communication is through sights and sounds—television and radio. Lamco Communications Inc. is an old company with a new name.

The firm traces its origins to a weekly newspaper called *Grit,* which first appeared in Williamsport on December 16, 1882. However, after little more than a year, the paper verged on collapse.

Dietrick Lamade, a German immigrant who had worked as a printer since he was 13, saw possibilities in *Grit* and purchased it. While the paper initially was sold only in and around Williamsport, Lamade's leadership and efforts resulted in its circulation expanding far beyond the West Branch Valley. Copies began to reach many states.

The newspaper incorporated on June 1, 1892, as Grit Publishing Company. Due to its growth, a four-story office building and printing plant were constructed at Third and William streets, and by the turn of the century *Grit's* circulation passed the 100,000 mark. Soon afterward the paper became available in every state, thereby making it a national publication.

In 1936 leadership of the firm was turned over to Lamade's sons: George R. was named president, and Howard J., vice-president. Ralph R. Cranmer became president in 1962.

Pioneering in offset printing in the early 1960s, *Grit* attracted interest in the printing industry both in the United States and abroad.

The firm in 1977 acquired Appalachian Broadcasting Corporation in Bristol, Virginia, which operates station WCYB-TV, an NBC affiliate and the leading station in the Tri-City area of Bristol-Kingston-Johnson City.

On March 31, 1981, the corporation sold its printing and publishing operations, as well as the name *Grit,* and changed its identity to Lamco Communications Inc.

In the next few years the Company purchased several companies. Pennsylvania Radio, Inc. - an AM/FM station in Williamsport, PA; a cable system located in Boyertown, PA and WXVT-TV (CBS affiliate) located in Greenville, Mississippi. These companies have since been sold.

Nationwide holdings were achieved with the purchase of KTXS-TV, Abilene, TX in December 1986; WCTI-TV, New Bern, NC in September 1993; and KRCR, Redding, CA in June 1996; all ABC affiliates.

Dietrick Lamade, publisher of the Grit *from 1882 to 1938. By the turn of the century the newspaper had grown from a local to a national publication.*

In 1936 the leadership of the company passed to Dietrick Lamade's sons. George R. (below) was named president and Howard J. (below right) became vice-president. Photos courtesy of Kaiden Kazanjian.

to the Lycoming County trash-collection campaign.

In March 1984 Lamco acquired Big River Broadcasting Company in Greenville, Mississippi—operator of WXVT-TV, a CBS affiliate serving the Mississippi Delta area.

During its years of producing a national newspaper or managing broadcast facilities, the corporation never lost interest in the city of its origin. Indeed, the company has been a vital part of Williamsport's progress through the years.

One of Lamco's proudest contributions is the 43-acre site it gave to Little League Baseball in 1959. The South Williamsport site is the international headquarters for that organization's worldwide program, as well as home for the annual Little League World Series. Little League proclaimed the stadium as Howard J. Lamade Field, in tribute to the benefactor who served on its board of directors for many years.

Another proud moment was in 1980 when Lycoming College named its new gymnasium for George R. Lamade, longtime president and publisher. The honor was in recognition of the company's strong financial backing over a long period of time, and of his personal support of the college's long-range development.

Lamco executives have served on the boards of many civic organizations, among them Lycoming United Way, Williamsport-Lycoming Chamber of Commerce, The Williamsport Hospital, Divine Providence Hospital, Guthrie Medical Center, James V. Brown Library, YMCA, YWCA, Park Home, Salvation Army, Blind Association, the Williamsport Home for the Aged, American Red Cross, and The Repasz Band.

They have also served as school directors, college trustees, and board members of the Williamsport Foundation, the Lycoming Foundation, Lycoming Industrial Development Authority, and the Lycoming County Planning Commission. In addition, the civic-minded businessmen have chaired many capital development drives for YWCA, YMCA, the library, and local hospitals.

Dietrick, George, Howard, J. Robert, and Howard Jr. have all been active in Freemasonry. Each has attained the honor of becoming a 33 Degree Mason.

Today, after 101 years of progress, Lamco looks to the future with eager anticipation to further growth and expansion. The closely held corporation maintains its headquarters in the Williamsport Building at 460 Market Street.

Officers of Lamco Communications Inc. are Marshall R. Noecker, President and CEO; Bernard G. Kolczynski, Vice President of Finance; James H. Lamade, Treasurer; Howard J. Lamade, Jr., Secretary; Robert J. Cunnion, Jr., Assistant Secretary.

The Lamco Communications Inc. Board of Directors includes (from left to right, top) Marshall R. Noecker, Andrew W. Stabler, Jr., Robert J. Cunnion, Jr., J. Robert Lamade, Bernard G. Kolczynski; (Bottom) Howard J. Lamade, Jr., James H. Lamade, and Ralph R. Cranmer.

CANDOR, YOUNGMAN, GIBSON & GAULT

Addison Candor

The law firm of Candor, Youngman, Gibson & Gault had its beginning when Addison Candor and C. (Cyrus) LaRue Munson went into partnership on October 1, 1875, at 46 Pine Street.

C. LaRue Munson

Addison Candor was born in Lewistown, Pennsylvania, in 1852. He earned his A.B. from Princeton in 1873, and subsequently read law at the office of Allen and Gamble —the most prominent law firm in Williamsport at the time. He was admitted to the Bar in 1875. Upon the death in 1900 of Lycoming County Judge John J. Metzger, the governor tendered the judgeship to Candor; however, he refused it and Max L. Mitchell was appointed.

Born in Bradford, New York, in 1854, C. LaRue Munson graduated from Episcopal Academy in 1871. The young man received his L.L.B. from Yale Law School in 1875, where he was a guest lecturer on legal practices for a number of years. President of the Pennsylvania Bar Association in 1902, Munson died 20 years later in China.

Both founders had sons who joined the organization after graduation from law school. Edgar Munson was awarded an A.B. from Yale in 1904 and an L.L.B. from Yale Law School in 1907. The latter year he was also admitted to the Bar. Prior to his death in 1930, Edgar Munson served as president of E. Keeler Company, vice-president of Williamsport Wire Rope Company, and was a trustee of The Savings Institution.

John Grafius Candor graduated in 1902 with an A.B. from Princeton and in 1905 with an L.L.B. from the University of Pennsylvania Law School. In addition to his position as president of The Williamsport Hospital, he was a member of the board of directors of the West Branch Bank and The Savings Institution.

John C. Youngman, Sr., who earned a B.S. in economics from the

Edgar Munson

John G. Candor

John C. Youngman, Sr.

Harry R. Gibson

University of Pennsylvania Wharton School in 1924, obtained his L.L.B. from Harvard Law School in 1927. Between 1932 and 1935 he served as district attorney of Lycoming County, and in 1943 formed a partnership with John G. Candor and Harry R. Gibson in the firm of Candor, Youngman and Gibson. Active in community affairs, Youngman was instrumental in procuring dikes for the Williamsport area and in the formation of the Williamsport Sanitation Authority. Now nestor of the Bar, he has practiced law for 57 years.

Receiving a B.S. from Lafayette College in 1928, Harry R. Gibson three years later was awarded an L.L.B. from Columbia University. The young attorney began his career in New York City with the firm of Robert H. Montgomery Law Offices, remaining there a year before returning to Williamsport. He has practiced law for 53 years and has been active in community affairs—notably as president of The Williamsport Hospital and as a director of the Northern Central Bank.

John C. Gault attained his A.B. from Bucknell University in 1939 and his L.L.B. from Dickinson Law School in 1942. A member of the FBI during World War II, he became a partner in the firm in 1948. Gault has served in the community with the Boy Scouts, as a trustee of The Savings Institution, and as a director of Commonwealth Bank and Trust Company, N.A.

John C. Youngman, Jr., was awarded a B.S. at Yale University in 1956, and earned an L.L.B. from Harvard Law School in 1959—at which time he joined the law firm. He also has been active in civic affairs, including serving as school director for 10 years, and leading the fight for fluoridation of the city's water supply.

John C. Gault

John C. Youngman, Jr.

TAMPELLA POWER

Like Williamsport, Tampella Power has its roots in the lumber era. The lumber industry was rebuilding after the devastating spring-1860 and September-1861 floods — which had not only sent thousands of logs and finished boards downstream, but had severely damaged the Susquehanna Boom and sawmills.

After these floods the Boom was purchased by Peter Herdic, Mahlon Fisher, and John C. Reading, who vastly strengthened and enlarged the operation. The expansion of the sawmills and other lumber-related industries along Williamsport's river was able to accelerate at a great pace, spurred by the demand for lumber that was being used in the Northeast's industrial expansion and in the Civil War. These sawmills and other plants needed boilers. The enterprise that eventually became Tampella Power was established through the ambition of several men to make a profit meeting that need.

Though sketchy and ambiguous information made an exact sequence of events impossible to document, some picture of the company's beginnings can be constructed. Isaac Barton is credited with a long-term contribution to the survival and growth of the firm in its first 65 years. One old document states, "On October 1, 1864, Mr. Barton came to Williamsport and with the two Maitlands and Joseph Heathcote, an Englishman, opened a boiler shop on the west side of West Street. Showing business as well as mechanical qualifications, he was made superintendent of the plant originally known as the firm of J. Heathcote and Company."

The economic problems following the Civil War, and apparently unwise and conflicting business practices and philosophies, put the young organization in such drastic financial straits that it endured years of bankruptcy crises; ultimately, on January 22, 1879, it was sold to F.R. Weed/First National Bank and to others. On March 30, 1883, Emily Keeler and Eleanor Keeler Lehman purchased parts of the properties, the main plant in particular, for $5,300 from Weed. Eleanor, the company's bookkeeper, was Emily's daughter and Barton's niece; he had married Susan A. Keeler. Eleanor acquired other parcels in the ensuing years, as did other individuals involved.

On March 16, 1888, as stated on the bill of sale, "Eleanor Keeler Lehman, the only member of said firm of E. Keeler & Company," sold the firm to the E. Keeler Company for $35,000. Mrs. Emily Keeler had died, and all her heirs quit-claimed any rights to the property in favor of Eleanor.

Who set policy and actually ran the operation over any particular span of time cannot be precisely pinpointed. One stabilizing individual who seems to have kept the plant functioning and productive was Isaac Barton. He was physically active until 1914 when he was confined to his home, though he remained involved as vice-president until his death on May 25, 1929, at the age of 91.

The production history of the corporation is also vague at its beginning. The first boilers were constructed using very primitive methods: Burly men used 30-pound sledgehammers to pound steel plates into top-ended cylinders to which ends were attached to make the body of the boiler.

In 1888, when the firm incorporated, there were 35 men employed manufacturing steam boilers, tanks, engine supplies, and plate work. About 1890 a division was set up to install piping systems for use with Keeler boilers, as well as a mill-supply wholesale outlet.

By 1906 the E. Keeler Company had grown to employ 175 men in 10,000 square feet in several buildings. In addition to manufacturing boilers it installed complete power plants, did steam fitting, heavy pipe work, plus heating and ventilating contract work. The wholesale/jobbing division carried the largest stock of mill and machinery supplies in the state outside of Pittsburgh and Philadelphia.

This photo of Keeler personnel surrounding a long drum boiler was printed and distributed on postcards in 1914 to commemorate the firm's 50th anniversary.

The federal government had become an extensive, continuing customer early in the firm's history. A large order in 1912 involved 12 water-tube boilers to operate in two permanent power plants on the Panama Canal. During World War I Keeler expanded to build boilers for government use and for firms producing war material. Wise investment of the profits, good management, and continued product development helped it to survive the heavy losses and operating deficits of the Depression.

During World War II Keeler manufactured boilers and furnaces for air force bases, training camps, depots, naval stations, and for many war-industry plants. In 1944 it received its largest single order up to that time when the U.S. Treasury Department placed a $2.5-million order for 80 easily transportable package boilers to produce 250 horsepower each in bombed-out cities desperately needing reliable power. The boilers were credited with helping to shorten the war and received a government citation. The Army Corps of Engineers diverted one Russia-bound boiler to help build an airstrip on Saipan, from which to bomb Tokyo.

In 1945 the wholesale-supply division was doing so well that it moved into a separate building at 335 West Third Street. That decade the success of the package-steam generators brought down costs but also reduced total sales volume. So success had to generate more innovations, which resulted in the D-Type boiler—a single-casing, pressure-fired unit that would account for half of Keeler's orders by 1971.

By its 100th anniversary in 1964, the corporation had operations in five major buildings on 13 acres. The annual payroll exceeded $1.5 million for over 300 employees.

In 1968 a $185,000 tube-bending shop was built at the east end of the boiler-manufacturing building. The same year the firm purchased the Faber Engineering Company of Norristown, Pennsylvania, which fabricated burners, and moved it to Williamsport. Keeler could then combine boilers and burners to provide new types of industrial burners in steam boilers, stills, kilns, and heaters.

From a family business serving Williamsport sawmills, the enterprise evolved into a corporation selling quality products throughout the world. There are Keeler boilers in Canada, Australia, Europe, South America, Russia, China, Iceland, Ireland, Cuba, the Philippines, and many other countries.

On February 23, 1982, the E. Keeler Company was acquired by Dorr-Oliver, which was founded over 75 years ago and was a wholly owned subsidiary of Standard Oil Company of Ohio.

The relationship began when Dorr-Oliver and Keeler cooperated in a Department of Energy project in the late 1970s in Shamokin to burn anthracite culm, a coal-preparation waste product, in a fluid-bed technology application. The project was so successful that Dorr-Oliver acquired Keeler.

The addition to the new product line of fluid-bed boilers, which should experience tremendous growth in the 1980s, has increased the firm's technical orientation and had required additional technical employees.

In July of 1987 Standard Oil sold the company to Con-Tor Holdings, Ltd. One year later it was purchased by the former management of the Dorr-Oliver Company. Keeler had become a small company selling a large capital product. On October 27, 1989 the company was acquired by Tampella Inc., a well established Finnish firm with forestry, paper products, mining machinery and recovery boiler divisions that dated back to the mid 1800's.

Tampella opened a recovery boiler sales and engineering office in Atlanta in 1984. Becoming aware of the advantages of manufacturing in the United States and the need for a firm with the background and boiler experience necessary to manufacture their quality product, they purchased Keeler/Dorr-Oliver. The former Pullman Power Product building at 2600 Reach Road in the Industrial Park area was purchased in February of 1990. The original plan was to manufacture package boilers at the West Street location and manufacture pressure part components for recovery and fluid bed boilers at the Industrial Park facility.

The shipping of an E. Keeler Co. boiler in 1890 prompted this celebration at what is now the corner of Third and William Streets.

CANADA DRY BOTTLING COMPANY, INC., OF WILLIAMSPORT

The multifranchise Canada Dry Bottling Company, Inc., of Williamsport is in its 46th year of operation. Here one of the over 50 employees checks a variety of soft drinks ready for distribution.

Since part of the A. Nardi & Sons produce business had been the distribution of Canada Dry beverages that were manufactured in New York State—packed in excelsior and shipped in wooden crates—two of the sons, Ralph A. Nardi, Sr., and Louis P. Nardi, obtained the franchise to bottle the drinks. On November 22, 1950, they established a new enterprise located at 517 Pine Street in a 5,000-square-foot building.

Ralph handled sales; Louis managed production; and their wives, Dorothy and Betty, shared the office work. Capacity was about 500 cases a day, and each of the 6,000 bottles had to be labeled one at a time by hand. Without modern forklifts, the heavy wooden crates and glass bottles had to be moved and stacked by hand. Within a year there were a dozen employees, one pickup truck, and two delivery trucks.

In 1952 the Hires franchise was acquired from Ray Thompson and moved to the Pine Street location. Hires remains the oldest brand of soft drink in the country. The 1950s also saw a steady growth in the pre-mix business for soda fountains.

Orange Crush brand was the next franchise to be acquired, in 1971, again from the Hires Company. A year later the Thomas Boyle Bottling Works was purchased, and Royal Crown Cola and Squirt were produced at its Rose Street plant until the new plant was opened in 1973 at 2120 Marydale Avenue.

Dr. Pepper, the second-oldest brand in the United States, was obtained in 1975. In the 1980s the firm became a jobber for Lipton Iced Tea, Yoo Hoo Chocolate Drink, Hawaiian Punch, and Welch's and Snapple brands.

In 1980 a distribution center was built in Lime Ridge (between Berwick and Bloomsburg) to service the Hazleton, Pottsville, and Shamokin areas.

Louis Nardi retired in 1969 and Ralph A. Nardi, Jr., purchased his share of the Canada Dry Bottling Company, Inc., of Williamsport. A year later the Canada Dry bottling plant in Hazleton closed, and distribution in the area was taken over by the Williamsport firm. At that time Ralph Jr., who had been working for the parent Canada Dry Corp. in Philadelphia, returned to Williamsport to join his father.

In its 46th year Canada Dry Bottling Company, Inc., of Williamsport has evolved into a multifranchise company with over 50 employees, 37 vehicles, and facilities of 42,000 square feet. A population of close to one million people in 12,000 square miles spread over 25 counties is served. Many of the consumers obtain their beverages from the several hundred street vending machines owned and serviced by the company, and from restaurants that use its fountain syrup and pre-mix.

From this distribution center at 2120 Marydale Avenue, the Canada Dry Bottling Company, Inc., of Williamsport services markets in a 25 county area.

ACKNOWLEDGMENTS

Our interest in this project is long standing and grows largely from our work with history students in our senior seminar at Lycoming College. Many have written fine papers on the Williamsport area that serve as sources for much of the story we tell. The papers we relied on most heavily were written by: Joseph Shannon, Michael Collins, Paul Roman, David Richards, Christine Updegraff, Werner Garben, William Inglis, David Wilson, Bonnie White, George Ebbert, Gregory McDonald, Frank Nunan, Robert Kane, John Protastio, Gerry Rhian, Mary Ann Smith, and Craig Weaver.

During the writing process itself and in securing pictures for the book, we have had the help of many knowledgeable and gracious individuals and institutions. Miriam Mix, John Troisi, Mary Winner Stockwell, James P. Bressler, Helen Youngman Carlson, Clifford A. Thomas, Thomas Rickey, Paul Bloom, Naomi Woolever, Amelia Mitchell, Paul Fullmer, Harry L. Rogers, Carl E. Stotz, Frank Cummings, Ann Williams, Founders Federal Savings and Loan, and The Williamsport *Sun Gazette* provided information, photographs, and family papers which have enhanced the book immeasurably. Special thanks must go to Marlin D. Fausey for his assistance in providing a plane for aeriel photography, and to Ralph E. Menne for his help with our color photography. The book was also enriched by the fine photographic collections at the James V. Brown Library, The Grit Publishing Company, and the Lycoming County Historical Museum. At the museum the D. Vincent Smith Collection was particularly useful. The successive directors of the museum, Andrew W. Grugan and Joseph L. Zebrowski, were especially helpful and kind. Paul G. Gilmore, William A. Turnbaugh, Marc L. Sheaffer, Joseph P. Laver, Andrew W. Grugan, and Richard L. Mix read copies of the manuscript, offered stylistic suggestions, and saved us from many errors in fact. Michael G. Roskin, our photographer, lent to the project a degree of artistry that is matched only by his patience with our perpetual desire for one more picture from one more angle. Madlyn Wonderlich, Nancy Morrett, and Judy Knittle at Lycoming College, who typed various versions of the manuscript, are not only skilled professionals but warm and agreeable co-workers. At Windsor Publications our editor Susan Wells was enormously supportive throughout the project.

BIBLIOGRAPHY

Anspach, Marshall R., ed. *Historical Sketches of the Bench and Bar of Lycoming County, Pennsylvania, 1795-1960.*Williamsport: Lycoming Law Association, 1961.

Beach, Nichols. *Atlas of Lycoming County, Pennsylvania.* Philadelphia: A. Pomeroy and Co., 1873.

Bey, Theophilus. *Williamsport Illustrated: A Presentation in Pictures from Original Photographs and in Text of the Places of Greatest Beauty and of the Religious, Educational, Financial, Manufacturing, and Commerce Factors that have made Williamsport one of the Leading Progressive Cities of the Nation.* Williamsport: Bey, 1910.

Blair, W.C., & McMath, J.B. *Condensed History of Williamsport.* Williamsport: Williamsport Gazette, 1873.

Blakesley, Alfred M. "The West Branch Front, A Summary of the War Effort in the West Branch Valley." Unpublished Paper, Williamsport: James V. Brown Library, 1945.

Boyd, Andrew, and Boyd, W. Harry. *Directory of Williamsport.* Pottsville: W.H. Boyd Co., 1867-1950.

Boyd, Julian, and Taylor, Robert J. *Susquehanna Company Papers.* Ithica: Cornell University Press, 1962-1971.

Building a Sense of Community. Williamsport: Williamsport Area School District, 1972.

Burgess, George H., and Kennedy, Miles C. *Centennial History of the Pennsylvania Railroad Company.* Philadelphia: Pennsylvania Railroad Co., 1949.

Burrows, John. *Sketch of the Life of General John Burrows: Furnished by Himself at the Request of His Numerous Relatives.* Williamsport: N. Bubb, 1917.

Clarke, W.P. *The Life and Times of the Honorable William Fisher Packer.* Williamsport: Lycoming Historical Society, 1937.

Collins, Michael. "A History of the Lycoming Hotel." Unpublished Paper, Williamsport: Lycoming College, 1983.

Coryell, Tunison. "Autobiographical Sketch of Tunison Coryell, 1791-1881." Williamsport: James V. Brown Library. (mimeograph)

DePol, John. *Lycoming College: Six Woodengravings Printed Directly from the Blocks in a Limited Edition.* Williamsport: Lycoming College, 1962.

Dugan, Jeffrey W. *The Bands of Williamsport Pennsylvania.* Unpublished Master's Paper, Pennsylvania State University, 1975.

Ebbert, George. "The Decision to Move Williamsport's City Hall." Unpublished Paper, Williamsport: Lycoming College, 1982.

Eckel, Edward Henry. *Chronicles of Christ Church Parish, Williamsport, PA., 1840-1896.* Williamsport: Press of the Gazette and Bulletin, 1910.

Faulkner, Harold U. *American Economic History.* New York: Harper & Brothers, 1938.

Fisher, Sydney George. *The Making of Pennsylvania.* Philadelphia: J.B. Lippencott Co., 1896.

Garben, Werner M. "The Rebuilding of St. Boniface Church." Unpublished Paper, Williamsport: Lycoming College, 1982.

Gazette and Bulletin. 1890-1955.

Goodrich, Carter. *Canals and American Economic Development.* New York: Columbia University Press, 1961.

Goodrich, Carter. *Government Promotion of American Canals and Railroads.* Westport: Greenwood Press, 1974.

Graves and Steinbarger. *Atlas of the City of Williamsport, PA., and Suburbs.* Philadelphia: Graves and Steinbarger, 1898.

Greater Williamsport Arts Council. *A Picture of Lycoming County, Vol. II.* Williamsport: Williamsport Arts Council, 1978.

The Grit. 1882-1984.

Harlow, Alvin F. *Old Towpaths: The Story of the American Canal Era.* New York: D. Appleton and Company, 1926.

Heitman, Francis. *Historical Register of the Officers of the Continental Army.* Rev. ed., Washington, D.C.: Rare Bookshop Publishing, 1914.

History of Lycoming County, Illustrated. Philadelphia: J.B. Lippincott and Co., 1876.

Homes and Heritage of the West Branch Valley. Williamsport: Junior League of Williamsport, Inc., 1968.

Humes, James C. *Sweet Dreams Tales of a River City.* Williamsport: Grit Publishing, 1966.

Hulslander, Steve. *From Lumberjacks to Smoke Stacks.* Williamsport: Williamsport Area School District, 1981.

Hunter, C.M. *Atlas of the City of Williamsport, PA.* Philadelphia: C.M. Hunter, 1888.

Huston, Charles. *Artwork of Williamsport.* Chicago: Parish, 1892.

Inglis, William. "The First National Bank of Williamsport." Unpublished Paper, Williamsport: Lycoming College, 1983.

Johnson, Allen, and Malone, Dumas, eds. *Dictionary of American Biography.* New York: Scribners, 1931.

Kane, Robert. "Annunciation Church: History of the Structural and Decorative Design 1889-1979." Unpublished Paper, Williamsport: Lycoming College, 1979.

Klein, Philip S., and Hoogenboom,Ari. *A History of Pennsylvania.* New York: McGraw-Hill, 1973.

Kulikoff, Allan. "The Progress of Inequality in Revolutionary Boston." *William and Mary Quarterly.* 3rd Ser. 28, (1971), pp. 375-412.

Lemon, James T., and Nash, Gary. "The Distribution of Wealth in Chester County, Pennsylvania, 1693-1802." *Journal of Social History.* 2 (1968) pp. 1-24.

Let's Take a Walk. The Greater Williamsport Community Arts Council and the Junior League of Williamsport, Inc., 1976.

Lycoming County Historical Preservation Plan. Prepared by Lycoming County Planning Commission, 1974.

Lycoming County Historical Society Journal. "Vanderbelt Papers." Williamsport: 1955-1984

Lycoming *Gazette.* 1807-1836.

McDonald, Gregory. "City Government and the Board of Trade: Progress and Reform in Williamsport, 1900-1917." Unpublished Honors Thesis, Williamsport: Lycoming College, 1980.

McMinn, J.H. *Complete History of First Baptist Church.* Williamsport: Williamsport Evening News, 1904.

Marsh, Warrern L., ed. "History of Covenant Central Presbyterian Church, Williamsport, PA; 1840-1952." Williamsport: James V. Brown Library, 1952. (mimeograph).

Meador, Yolanda, ed. *Loyalsock: The Evolution of A Modern Township.* Bicentennial Committee of Loyalsock Township.

Meginnes, John F. *Genealogy and History of the Hepburn Family of the Susquehanna Valley, With Reference to Other Families of the Same Name.* Williamsport: Gazette and Bulletin Printing, 1894.

Meginnes, John F. *History of Lycoming County Including Its Aboriginal History.* Chicago: Brown, 1892.

Meginnes, J.F., ed. *Resources and Industries of the City of Williamsport and the County of Lycoming.* Williamsport: Williamsport Gazette, 1886.

Minutes of the Provincial Council of Pennsylvania from the Organization to the Termination of the Proprietary Government. Harrisburg: Theophilus Fenn, 1852.

Motter, Alton M., ed. *Religion in Lycoming County.* Williamsport: United Churches of Lycoming County, 1982.

Murray, J.F. "History of the War Work of the Public Schools of Williamsport." Unpublished Paper, Williamsport: James V. Brown Library, 1920.

Nunan, Frank. "Little League Baseball: A Study of Its Growth and Effects in America." Unpublished Paper, Williamsport: Lycoming College, 1979.

Pennsylvania Archives. Philadelphia and Harrisburg: Joseph Severns, 1896-1935.

Pennsylvania Writers Projects of the W.P.A. *A Picture of Lycoming County.* Williamsport: Commissioners of Lycoming County, 1939.

Pessen, Edward. *Jacksonian America: Society, Personality, and Politics.* Rev. ed. Homewood: Dorsey Press, 1978.

Pierce, Edward L. "Lycoming County in the Civil War." Unpublished Master's Thesis, Pennsylvania State University, 1934.

Plankenhorn, William Frederick. "Geographic Study of the Growth of Greater Williamsport." Unpublished Ph.D. dissertation, Pennsylvania State University, 1957.

Protasio, John. "Italian Americans in Williamsport." Unpublished Paper, Williamsport: Lycoming College, 1979.

Repasz Band. *Repasz Band Williamsport, PA., The Oldest Band in America.* Williamsport: Grit Publishing, 1915.

Rhian, Terry. "Williamsport's Economic Development During the Canal Period, 1820-1850." Unpublished Paper, Williamsport: Lycoming College, 1980.

Richards, David. "The 109th Infantry Regiment in the Battle of Huertgen Forest." Unpublished Paper, Williamsport: Lycoming College, 1982.

Rick, William F. *A Brief History of St. Marks Ev. Lutheran Church: The Pioneer Church of Lutheranism in this City 1852-1890.* Williamsport: Gazette and Bulletin Printing, 1896.

Roman, Paul. "Rationing in Williamsport During World War II." Unpublished Paper, Williamsport: Lycoming College, 1980.

Rosenberger, Homer T. *The Philadelphia and Erie Railroad: Its Place in American Economic History.* Potomac: The Fox Hills Press, 1975.

Russell, Helen H. *The Tiadaghton Tale: A History of the Area and Its People.* Compiled by Carol F. Baker. Williamsport: Scaife's Valley Press, 1975.

Russell, Mary L. "History of Music of Williamsport." Unpublished Master's Thesis, Pennsylvania State University, 1957.

Schlesinger, Arthur M., Jr. *The Age of Jackson.* Boston: Little Brown, 1945.

Shannon, Joseph. "Impact of Industrialization on the Wealth Distribution of Williamsport." Unpublished Paper, Williamsport: Lycoming College, 1983.

Sipes, William D. *Pennsylvania Railroad: Its Origin, Construction, Condition, and Connections.* Evansville: Unigraphic, Inc., 1975.

Stotz, Carl E., with Baldwin, M.W. *At Bat with the Little League.* Philadelphia: Macrae Smith, 1952.

Taber, Thomas T., III. *Sunset Along Susquehanna Waters.* Williamsport: Lycoming Printing Company, Inc., 1972.

Taylor, George R. *The Transportation Revolution.* New York: Rinehart, 1951.

Turnbaugh, William A. *Man, Land, and Time.* Evansville: Unigraphic, Inc., 1977. Published for the Lycoming County Historical Society, Williamsport

Turnbaugh, William A. "Six Cheers and a Volley." Unpublished

Manuscript, 1969.
U.S. Bureau of the Census. "Population of the Second Census of the United States 1800." Roll 41, Pennsylvania, Vol. 7, National Archives: Washington, D.C., 1957.
U.S. Bureau of the Census. "Population of the Thirteenth Census of the United States, 1910." Roll 1372-1373 Lycoming County, National Archives: Washington, D.C.
United States Department of Commerce. *Sixteenth Census of the United States; 1940 Population.* Washington, D.C.: Government Printing Office, 1942.
United States Department of Commerce. *Report on Vital and Social Statistics in the United States at the Eleventh Census, 1890.* Washington, D.C.: Government Printing Office, 1896.
U.S. Government Printing Office. *Heads of Families at the First Census of the United States Taken in the Year 1790, Pennsylvania.* Baltimore: Genealogical Publishing Co., 1977.
Updegraff, Christine. "The Transformation of Farming in Lycoming County." History Internship, Lycoming County Planning Commission, 1975.
Wallace, Paul A. *Pennsylvania: Seed of a Nation.* New York: Harper & Row, 1962.
Weaver, Craig. "Internship on Michael Ross." Unpublished Paper, Williamsport: Lycoming College, 1976.
White, Bonnie. "Women in Employment During World War II: The Nation and Williamsport." Unpublished Paper, Williamsport: Lycoming College, 1979.
"Williamsport Tax Records 1808-1844." Lycoming County Historical Society, Williamsport, PA.
Williamsport Junior League. *The West Fourth Street Story.* Williamsport: Grit Publishing, 1975.
Williamsport-Lycoming Chamber of Commerce. "Minutes and Annual Reports of the Williamsport Chamber of Commerce, 1927-1937." Williamsport.
Williamsport-Lycoming Chamber of Commerce. "Minutes and Annual Reports of the Williamsport Board of Trade and Chamber of Commerce, 1919-1927." Williamsport.
Williamsport-Lycoming Chamber of Commerce. "Minutes of the Committee of 100, 1935-1937." Williamsport
Wilson, David S. "The History of the North-Central Chapter of the Society for Pennsylvania Archaeology." Unpublished Paper, Williamsport: Lycoming College, 1980.
Wilson, William B. *History of the Pennsylvania Railroad Company.* Philadelphia: H.T. Coates & Co., 1895.
Woolever, Naomi L. "The Street Railway Era in Williamsport, PA." *The Bulletin of the National Railway Historical Society.* Vol. 40, No. 4, 1975, pp. 35-48.
Yount, Paul L. *An Historical Survey of St. Mark's Lutheran Church of Williamsport, PA.* Williamsport: Grit Publishing, 1927.
Zamarra, Jacqueline. "The Water Company of Williamsport, Pennsylvania: From Private Ownership to Municipal Acquisition." Unpublished Paper, Williamsport: Lycoming College, 1981.

INDEX

PARTNERS IN PROGRESS INDEX

Alcan Cable 154
Anchor/Darling Valve Company 153
Canada Dry Bottling Company, Inc. 170
Candor, Youngman, Gibson & Gault 166-167
Eureka Paper Box Company, Inc. 155
George E. Logue Inc. 156-157
James Meyer Company 162
Keystone Filler & Mfg. Co. 152
Lamco Communications, Inc. 164-165
Lycoming College 163
Northern Central Bank 160-161
Pennsylvania College of Technology 158
Susquehanna Health System 144-147
Tampella Power 168-169
Textron Lycoming 148-151
WWPA/Williamsport Radio Corporation 159

GENERAL INDEX
Italicized numbers indicate illustrations

A
Academic Center (Lycoming College) *104*, 105
Alcan Cable Company *116*, 117
Allegheny Front 10, 11
Allegheny Plateau 14
Almshouse 64, 66
American Revolution 20, 21, 26
Annunciation Roman Catholic Church *52*, 53, 54, 71, 74
Anthony, Joseph B. 34, 38
Anti-Masonry 29, 31
Appalachian Mountains 9, 20
Appalachian Plateau 9
Armstrong, James 34
Articles of Confederation 19
Athletic Stadium 120
Avco Lycoming Company 84, 115
Aviation Corporation, Lycoming Division *103*

B
Bald Eagle Art League 129
Bald Eagle Creek 11
Bald Eagle Mountain 9, *10*, 11, 128
Banger, George 37
Bank of the United States 34
Battle of the Bulge 101
Beautiful Susquehanna Trail, The (pamphlet) 90
Beech Valley School 117
Beiter, Bernardine 72, *73*
Beltway. *See* Susquehanna Beltway
Beth Hashalom (temple) 51
Bethlehem Steel 115
Bethune-Douglass Community Center 109
Big Runaway 21
Big Water Mill 37, 39
Bishop Neumann High School 117
Board of Health 64, 66
Board of Public Works 64
Board of Trade, The 63, 64, 70, 71, 84, 90, 97
Bonus Army *80*
Boost Business Caravan *132*, 133
Bowman and Company, B.C. 47
Bowman Field 130
Brandon, Joseph 38
Brandon Park 54, 109, 120, *121, 126*
Brandon Park Bandshell 77
Bressler, James P. 18
Bull Run 19
Burrows, John 38

C
Campbell, Francis C. 38
Campbell, Jane Hepburn 38
Campbell, Mary Jane 38
Canals 32, 33, *34*, 35
Canal Street Urban Renewal Project 107
Canfield Island *18*
Carl, Kenneth E. 119
Carroll House 115
Carter, Jimmy *109*
Center City Mall 108, 115
Charles II 17
Chianelle, Michael 74
Chickasaw Indians 17
Christ Episcopal Church 77
Cillo, Peter 74
Citizens Responsibility Committee 117
Citizens Traction Company 67
City Hall *62*, 63
Civic Ballet Company 129
Civic Choir (chorus) 129
Civil War 41
Civil Works Administration *96*
Clarke Building 120, *121*
Cochran, J. Henry 63
Colony of Pennsylvania 17
Committee of 100 97, 98
Committee of Public Safety 81
Community Mental Health Center for Lycoming-Clinton Counties 120
Community Theater League 129
Community Trade Association 98, 113
Confair, Z.H. 113
Congregation Ohev Shalom 106, *107*
Consistory Plat *94, 95*
Cord (automobile) 86
Coryell, Tunison 29, 33, 38, *39*
Covenant Presbyterian Church 76
Crash of 1929 94
Crawford, John 37
Culver, Eber 51, 57, 62
Curbstone Market *84, 85*

D
D-Day 101
Darling Valve and Manufacturing Company 103
Debs, Eugene V. 78
Delaware Indians 17, 20
Demmien, Bob *18*
Demorest Manufacturing Company 61
Dickinson Junior College 117
Dickinson Seminary 30, 51, 52, *53*, 94
Diston Manufacturing Company 61
Divine Providence Hospital 120
Dodge, Charles 37
Dodge, John 37
Dodge Mills *46*, 47
Dongan, Thomas 17
Donley, Hugh 34
Drama Workshop 129
DuBoistown *10*, 47, 56
Duesenberg (automobile) 86
Dutch Hill 71

E
Eagle Hotel *3*, 4
Eagles Mere 79
Earhart, Amelia 89
East End Traction Company 67
Electricity 56
Eleventh Regiment of Pennsylvania Volunteers 41
Ellis, William 23
Elmira and Williamsport Railroad 34
Emery, William 124
Emery House *24*
Emmanuel Baptist Church 117
Erie Canal 32
Ertel, Allen *115*
Exposition Building *79*

F
Faires, Robert 30, 38
Faith Tabernacle Christian Academy 117
Federal Building 114, *115*
Federal Emergency Relief Administration 97
Federal Surplus Commodities Corporation 94, *95*
Festival of the Arts 129
First Baptist Church 32
First Evangelical Church 99
First National Bank of Williamsport 64, *65*
Fischer, John 129
Fischer, Jonas 71, 78
Fisher, Mahlon *44*, 54, 57
Flood Control 109, *110, 111*
Floods 14, 15, 44, 54; of 1889, 57, *58*; of 1935-1936, *99, 100*, 109, 110
Folded Appalachian Mountains 9
Foresman, Seth 66
Forrest Inn 79
Fort Muncy *20*
Fort Sumter 41
Founders Federal Savings and Loan Association 125
Freedom Hill 30
French and Indian War 17
Furniture Manufacturing 48

G
Gamble, James 54
Gamble, Mary White 124
Gazette and Bulletin (newspaper) 79
Gehron, Harold *130*
Gehron, Jimmy *130*
Genetti Lycoming Hotel *104*, 105
Gesang Verein Harmonia Society 71, 129
Gibson, George 21
Gibson, Harry R. 120
Grant, Ulysses S. 41
Great Depression 81, 94, *95*
Golden Strip 115
Grampian Hill 30
Grampian Hills Development Company *93*
Greevy, Thomas H. 47
Grit (newspaper) 51, 64, *65*, 79
Grit Award for Meritorious Community Service 109
Growers Association Market 84
Grower's Market 115

H
Hall, John B. 37
Hand, Horace 129
Hartley, Thomas 13
Hartman, Daniel W. 120
Hepburn, Andrew D. 26, 38
Hepburn, Samuel 38
Hepburn, Sarah 38
Hepburn, William 22, *23*, 26, 27, 38
Hepburn Street Dam *131*
Hepburn Street Pumping Station *110*, 111
Herdic, Peter 37, *44*, 45, 46, 47, 50, 61, 123, 124
Herdic House 40, *45*, 46
Hermance, A.D. 49
Hershberger, Harold D. *108*
Hiawatha (riverboat) *77, 126*, 131
Hills, Mary 120
Holmes Silk Mill *75*, 103
Home for the Friendless 54
Homesteading Program 107
Hope Enterprises, Inc. 108, 120
Housel, Osborne 129
Howard J. Lamade Stadium 126
Huertgen Forest 101
Hughes, Daniel *30*
Hughes, Henry 34
Hughesville 56
Huling, James 26
Hunter, Samuel 21
Hurricane Agnes 111, 112, 113

I
Imperial (automobile) *64*
Imperial Motor Company 64
Imperial Teteques 120
Industrial Park 117
Industrial Properties Corporation
Industrial Revolution 41
Influenza epidemic 86
Iroquois Indians 17

J
Jackson, Andrew 27, 29
Jaysburg 21, 22, 23
J.K. Mosser Company 89
Johnson, Lyndon B. 109
Junction Traction Company 67

K
"Keds" 89
Keeler Company 63
Keystone Shortway Association 10
113, 114
Kirby, Daniel P. *115*
Klump Academic Center *70*
Knight, Charles *75*
Knights of Columbus 84
Know-Nothing Party 30
Krouse, Charles C. 84, 97

L
L.L. Stearns 48, *50*
Lamade, Dietrick 51, *52*, 64
Lamoka Indians 17
Landro, Domenica 74
Laurentian Indians 17, 18
Leader, George M. 114
Lee, Robert E. 41
Leederman, Fred 64
Leni Lenape Indians 17, 20
Lentz, George W. 37
Lepley, George *113*
Liberty Bonds 84
"Little Hollywood" 74
Little League Baseball *126, 127*, 130
Little League World Series 130
Lockard, Joseph L. 101
Long, John W. 118
Long Administration Building 120
Long Reach 11, 15
Low, Charles 26
Loyal Plaza 115
Loyalsock Creek 11, 25
Loyalsock Creek Village *12*, 13
Loyalsock Township 19, *106, 107*,
Lumber Industry 10, 14, 15, 47, 48, 61
Lycoming College 25, 105, 108, 116, 120, *121*
Lycoming College Arena Theater
Lycoming College Choir 129
Lycoming County Bar Association
Lycoming County Court House 17
31, 50, 86, *87*, 114, *122*
Lycoming County Fair Grounds 7

.ycoming County Historical Museum 19, *27*
.ycoming County Medical Society 37, 54
.ycoming County Planning Commission 10
.ycoming County Sunday School Association 30
.ycoming Creek 11, 13, 14, 22, 25, 32
.ycoming Engine 102
.ycoming Foundry and Machine Company 84, 86
.ycoming *Gazette* (newspaper) 25, 33, 38, 41
.ycoming Hotel *90*
.ycoming Mall 115
.ycoming Mfg. Company 86, 97, 102, 133
.ycoming Opera House 54, 129
.ycoming Rubber Company 89, 96
.ycoming United Fund *108*

M
McClure, Robert 27
McDonald, Peyton D. *108*
McElrath, Robert 24
McIver, Walter G. 129
McKinley, William B. 63
Madame Montour's Village 19
Mahaffey, Laura Valeria *72*
Main Street Project 107
Mankey Decorative Works 49
Mansel, James 63
Market Square 34, 57, *58, 60,* 61, 67, *125*
Market Street Bridge *8,* 9, *68, 69, 112,* 113
Market Street Railroad Station *82, 83*
Marine Band 81
Mason-Dixon Line 19
Masons 30, 31
Mater Dolorasa Parish 74
Maynard, John 123
Maynard and Company, Guy W. 47
Maynard Street Bridge 56, *92*
Max C. Miller Training Center 120
Memorial Park 92, 130
Methodist Episcopal Church 31, 32
Miller, Max C. *118,* 120
Millionaires Row 52, 53, 54
Million Dollar House" 54, *57*
Mission Chapel 76
Mitchell, Percy David *109*
Montoursville 56
Mosquito Creek 26
Mountain Beach *97*
Mueller, Otto R. *110,* 111
Muir, Malcolm 114
Muncy 9, 19, 20
Muncy Creek 11
Muncy Farms 21
Muncy Historical Museum 20
Muncy Valley 20
Municipal Building *62,* 63
Munson, Cyrus La Rue 61, *63*
Munson Lumber Company 63
Mussina, Jacob 34

N
Nardi, Peter 74
National Guard 81, *82,* 83
New Deal 98
Newer Appalachian Mountains 9
New School Branch (Presbyterian Church) 32
New York World's Fair 113
Noyes, Charles E. 113

O
Older Appalachian Mountains 9
Otto, John 37

P
Packer, William Fisher 33, *34,* 38
Panic of 1837 34, 39
Parkes, George H. 98
Pearce, John J. 30
Pearl Harbor 101
Penn Street Armory *6,* 7
Pennsylvania Association for Retarded Children 120
Pennsylvania Board of Education 119
Pennsylvania Canal System 33
Pennsylvania Guild of Craftsmen, Williamsport Chapter 129
Pennsylvania Railroad Station 46, *63*
Pennsylvania Medical Society 37
Pennsylvania Turnpike 113
Perkins, James 37, 44
Piatt, William, Jr. 34
Pickelner, William *108*
Pine Creek 11, 13, 15
Pine Street Methodist Church *31*
Plankenhorn, Frank E. 93
Plum Thicket Massacre 20, 21
Population 10, 13, 24, 25, 26, 36, 63, 91, 101, 105
Post, Leo J. 120
Preachers' Aid Society 53
Presbyterian Church 31
Prior and Salada Company 115
Progressive Movement 61
Protestant Episcopal Church 32

R
Ralston, Robert 34
Reading, John 44
Recreation 94, 130, 131
Red Cross 84
Reed, C.A. 96
Reed Company 89, 103
Reeder, Paul D. *111*
Reedy, John 74
Reformed Church 32
Relief Garden Show *94, 95*
Repasz Band 41, 81
Repasz-Elks Band 120
Rhone, Kenneth D. 113
Rider, Thomas J. 97
Ritner, Joseph 34
Rizzo, Mary 74
Rizzo, Tony 74
"Roaring Twenties" 86
Roesen, Severein 125
Roosevelt, Franklin D. 98
Rose Valley School 117
Ross, Elizabeth 26
Ross, Margaret 26
Ross, Michael *21,* 22, 23, 25, 26, 131
Ross, William 23
Ross Park *62*
Rotch, Annie 30
Rowley, E.A. 49
Royal Braid Company 61
Russell, James 17
Russell, William 23
Russell Inn *16,* 17, 23

S
Saint Ann's School 117
Saint Boniface Roman Catholic Church 32, 40, *69,* 71, 72, 120
Saint John's Chapel 77
Saint Joseph's High School 117
Saint Mark's Lutheran Church 32
Saint Mary's High School 117
Saint Patrick's Day Flood 15
Salvation Army 84
Savings Institution of Williamsport 63
Sawdust War 47, 48, 59, 74
Sawyer Park 66
Schneebeli, Herman T. 114, *115*
Schneider, Elizabeth 74
Schneider, Louis 74
School of Hope *118,* 120
Scott, J.M. 51
Seaman, Larry 88
Second Presbyterian Church 32, 76
Seneca Indians 17
Shawnee Indians 17
Shellenberger, Thomas H. 129
Shenks Ferry Indians 17, *18, 19*
Sheraton Motor Inn *104,* 105
Shortway 113
Sinclair Station *88*
Sisters of Christian Charity 120
Slaughter, Mary *76,* 77
Sloan, Samuel 122
Slough, Matthias 21
Smith, D. Vincent *78*
Social Gospel 75, 76
Socialist Party 78
Society for Pennsylvania Archeology *18*
South Side Traction Company 67, 68
South Williamsport *8,* 9, *10, 14,* 46, 47
Sports 130, 131
Stearns, George L., III 97
Stearns, L.L. 48, *50*
Stenger, Jay 129
Stockwell, Mary Winner 72
Stotz, Carl E. *130*
Stroehmann's Bakery 71
Stull, Mary *110,* 111
South Williamsport 77
Sullivan, P.F. 71
Sunbury *Public Inquirer* 38
Sun-Gazette (newspaper) 129
Sunset Park 92, *93*
Susquehanna Beltway *8,* 9, 114
Susquehanna Boom Company 37, 43, 44
Susquehanna Boom Festival 131
Susquehanna Canoe Club *92,* 93
Susquehanna Indians 17
Susquehanna River *6,* 7, 9, 11, 13, 14, 15
Susquehanna River, North and West Branch Telegraph Company 34
Susquehanna Section 11
Susquehanna State Park *130, 131*
Susquehanna Valley Orchestra 129
Sutton, Amariah 32
Sylvan Dell Park *77,* 79, *126*
Sylvania Electric Products Company, Inc. 103

T
Taft, William Howard 78
Tallman, Jeremiah 34
Telephone Service 56
Tinsman, Garrett 37
Tinsman, Peter 37
Tourism 90
Trinity Episcopal Church 51, 53
Trinity Episcopal Parish *123*
Troisi, Domenic 72, *73*
Turnbaugh, William 11

U
Ulman Opera House 54, *125,* 129
Underground Railroad 29, 30, 34
United States Rubber Company 96
United States Sanitary Commission 42
Updegraff, Abraham 29, *30, 72*
Updegraff, Thomas 50

V
Vallamont Traction Company 67, 68
Valley Iron Works 48
Valley View Associates 106, 107
Vanderbelt, Mary 38
Vanderbelt, Peter 26, 27
Van Feris, C.P. 64
Van Horne, Espy 26
Van Horne, Henrietta 26
Vannucci, Americus 74
Victory Arch *83*
Vienna International Exhibition 48
VonNeida, Willard G. 78

W
Wakenhut Building 100, 101
Walker, Annie Weightman 51
Wallis, Joseph 34
Walnut Street High School 70
Watsontown High School 119
Watsontown Plan 119
Weightman Block *50, 51*
Wertz Student Center 120, *121*
West Branch *Beobachter* (German newspaper) 43
West Branch Bank 29
West Branch Canal 25, 32, *33,* 34, 39, 112
West Branch School 117
West Branch Valley *8,* 9, 11, 13, 14, 20
West Edwin Street Urban Renewal Project 107
West End Traction Company 67
Whig Party 30
White, Henry 37
White, John 37
White Kitchen Market *84*
Wildwood Cemetery 37
Williams, Joseph 23
Williams, Samuel N. 63
Willimasport Academy 25
Williamsport Academy of Music 54
Williamsport Airport *88,* 89
Williamsport and Elmira Railroad 30
Williamsport Area Community College 70, 118
Williamsport Area School District 117, 130
Williamsport Bridge Company 30
Williamsport Chamber of Commerce 91, 96, 97, 98, 129
Williamsport Christian School 117
Williamsport City Directory 74
Williamsport Community Arts Council 129
Williamsport Federation of Churches 77
Williamsport Fire Department *90*
Williamsport Foundation 108
Williamsport Furniture Company 103
Williamsport Gas Company 36
Williamsport High School *71,* 98, 105, 118, *119*
Williamsport Hospital 54, 94, 108, 120
Williamsport Hotels Company 90
Williamsport Imperial Teteques 120
Williamsport Jaycees 131
Williamsport-Lycoming Chamber of Commerce 62, 108, 111, 117, 126, 131
Williamsport Masonic Lodge 31
Williamsport Plan 98
Williamsport Players 129
Williamsport Recreation Commission 7
Williamsport Retraining School 98
Williamsport School Board 118

Williamsport Steam Company 56
Williamsport Symphony Orchestra 120, 129
Williamsport Technical Institute 118
Williamsport Water Company 30, 36
Williamsport Wire Rope Company 61, 84, 96, 103
Williamsport Writers Forum 129
Wilson, William 26, 34
Winter, Eleanor 23
Winter, William 21
Winters, Michael J. 66
Wolf, George 33
Wolf, Henry M. 51
Wolfe, Charles D. 67
Wolfe, Chester D. *11*
Wood, James W. 50
Wood, Thomas 117
Woodward, Cornelius 124
Woodward, John Vanderbelt 124
Woolverton, Runyon 37
Works Progress Administration *96,* 98
World War I *80,* 81, 83
World War II 81, 101, 103, 105
Woxman, Clive R. 120
W.T. Grant Company 115

X,Y,Z
Yankee-Pennamite Wars 19
Youngman, George Washington 56
Youngman, John C. 109
Youngman Estate *56*
YWCA 57
Ziegler, Paul 129